PRAISE FOR THE PRIVATE TUT(

Amy Lucas brings more than a decade of ι   ͜   ͙ͫ the ͙͙͜͠ levels of the tutoring/test prep industry to this production. Starting with math vocabulary and then offering a discussion of the range of SAT problems from algebra to geometry to functions, this series offers the student the broadest coverage of the SAT math section. VERDICT: Highly recommended for students facing the SATs.

Library Journal, Math section review

In stark contrast to the "teacher in front of a chalk board"... the presentation is personal, conversational, relaxed, and effective.

Peggy Dominy, Liaison Librarian, Drexel University, Philadelphia, PA

I was really impressed! It gave me insight of an easier way to look at a problem... one of the best study skills books I've come across.

Amneris González, Instructional Support Svcs., Secondary Math, LAUSD

Library collections serving high school students as well as homeschoolers seeking instruction, practice, and basic standardized test-taking tips for the Math SAT will find this series an essential purchase.

School Library Journal, Starred review, Math section

Lucas divides the test into four categories—test numbers and operations, geometry and measurements, algebra and functions, and statistics and probability—and further breaks these categories into understandable chapters so that the complexity of both the subject and the test is reduced. Ten chapters provide step-by-step instructions and simplify concepts by utilizing illustrated sample problems as well as comprehensive drills at the end of each lecture.

Linda M. Teel, East Carolina University, Greenville, NC

I like the informal approach that the author uses to get on the student's level about the topics. Identifying each example and exercise with its relative difficulty also gives students a better sense of what to expect on the exam... well done; the portions where Amy gives her explanations with graphics are well thought out and produced...

David Hammett, Math Department Chair, Oakwood School, Los Angeles

The three different techniques for reading based on ability is an amazing idea. I have never seen it addressed this way and it is so important. The sample readings were excellent... the one on video games was particularly good... the answer explanations are great and are key to a student's success. If they can understand their error it will help immensely.

Kevin Murchie, teacher, James A. Garfield Senior High School, Los Angeles, CA

The tutorial on the essay section covers the important points in a clear and concise manner… the technique she employs will produce results… it works.

Nick Garrison, private tutor, Greenwich, CT

This set of two DVDs and a workbook walks the viewer through the writing component of the SAT and offers advice on how to approach the test. Narrator and tutor Amy Lucas is attractive and vivacious… her delivery makes the videos easy to watch.

Rosemary Arneson, Univ. of Mary Washington Lib., Fredericksburg, VA

Lucas clearly states that she is coaching viewers on test-taking strategies, not teaching them general rules of grammar. Her examples are lucid and the suggestions consistent with those offered by other standardized test guides… VERDICT: Watching these DVDs and completing the workbook will not make the viewer a great writer, but the processes will help a student gain confidence in the writing skills required by the SAT.

Library Journal, Writing section review

…she has an expressive style that should hold the attention of students. All incorrect responses are explained clearly. There are easy-to-follow tips for writing the essay as well as sample essays that received high and low scores.

Ellen Frank, School Library Media Specialist, Jamaica High School, NY

Students looking for a comprehensive review of the Writing portion of the SAT will find this program very helpful, especially since they can select specific areas in which they need improvement.

School Library Journal, Writing section review

Private Tutor

Your Complete SAT Writing Prep Course with Amy Lucas

SAT® is a registered trademark of the College Entrance Examination Board. Neither The College Board nor The Educational Testing Service (ETS) was involved in the production and do not endorse this product.

For additional test prep coaching, contact Amy at www.testpreptutor4you.com.

Written by Amy Lucas
Layout and design by Kathy Cotter

All inquiries should be addressed to:
Private Tutor
15124 Ventura Blvd., Suite 206
Sherman Oaks, CA 91403
tel: 818.508.1296 • fax: 818.508.9076
info@PrivateTutorSAT.com

More SAT tutorial books and DVDs are available at www.PrivateTutorSAT.com.

PRINTED IN THE UNITED STATES OF AMERICA
9 8 7 6 5 4 3 2 1

Table of Contents

Introduction

Hi, I'm Amy Lucas and I'm going to be walking you through the SAT Writing section, which is made up of an essay and multiple-choice questions that test your ability to identify grammar errors and improve grammar usage. I have included an overview of technique for each of the different types of multiple-choice questions, a parts of speech refresher, the 19 grammar rules the SAT tests accompanied by over 80 practice problems, and an essay section that includes a fool-proof formula and sample essays.

The SAT Writing section is my favorite portion of the SAT because it is the easiest to improve. Learn the 19 grammar rules and you can get a perfect score on the grammar portion of the SAT. The same rules are tested over and over again in pretty much the SAME WAY EVERY TIME. You only need to know the grammar rules I give you. If you see what you think may be an error on the SAT that wasn't covered in this book, then chances are it's not an error at all.

Treat this program like a class you're taking in school. You are learning SAT grammar. I might teach you things that contradict what your schoolteachers have told you about essay writing or grammar rules. For instance, many teachers have drilled into students' brains never to start a sentence with the word "because." On the SAT, however, it is perfectly acceptable to start a sentence with "because."

So who are the Mensa geniuses behind the SAT? The SAT is owned by the College Board, but administered by the Educational Testing Service. I'm going to refer to the test makers as ETS. Many SAT experts will tell you that ETS is evil and out to get you. If that motivates you – use it! I personally think ETS could get a heck of a lot trickier. Either way, I'm here to help you master the game.

STRUCTURE

The Writing portion of the SAT is made up of 49 multiple-choice questions and an essay. The first section of the SAT is always the essay. You have 25 minutes to write an essay on a given assignment. The first multiple-choice grammar section can fall anywhere between sections 2 and 9 of the SAT (usually it shows up in sections 3 through 7). You have 25-minutes to complete this multiple-choice section made up of 35 questions: 11 Sentence Correction questions, 19 Error ID questions, and 6 Improving Paragraphs questions. The last section of the SAT is always a 10-minute multiple-choice grammar section made up of 14 Sentence Correction questions.

EXPERIMENTAL SECTION

You might end up with two 25-minute multiple-choice writing sections on the SAT. If this is the case, one of those grammar sections is the experimental section. Leave it to ETS to make you do an extra 25-minute Math, Writing, or Critical Reading section that doesn't count towards your score and makes the test a good 3 hours and 45 minutes. ETS is using you as a guinea pig to test out future SAT questions. The experimental section does not affect your score in any way, but you still have to do it because you won't know which of the two 25-minute sections is the experimental section.

CONTENT

ESSAY

When you open your test booklet, Section 1 hits you with an essay. Within a box will be another box that contains a prompt and then the assignment you are expected to address. Take a look:

Think carefully about the issue presented in the following excerpt and the assignment below.

> There are many who believe that it is up to a country's government to solve the problems of its nation. After all, shouldn't a governing body deal with large-scale issues, such as the rising homeless population or unsafe road conditions? And yet, by placing so much of our nation's fate in the hands of the government, we have weakened our independence and self-sufficiency.

Assignment: <u>Should people be more proactive about resolving problems that affect their communities or nation</u>? Plan and write an essay in which you develop your point of view on this issue. Support your position with reasoning and examples taken from your reading, studies, experience, or observations.

MULTIPLE-CHOICE QUESTIONS

The multiple-choice questions are made up of *Sentence Corrections*, *Error IDs*, and *Improving Paragraphs*.

The Writing section is supposed to be arranged in terms of order of difficulty, but it is a bit more randomized than that. You can be assured that the first couple of Sentence Corrections are easy and the last few Sentence Corrections are trickier. The same goes for the Error Ids: The first few are a breeze, and the last several are pretty tough. But from there, ETS may scatter easy, medium, and hard questions throughout. The Improving Paragraphs section is made up of easy and medium problems; pace yourself and make sure you have enough time to complete the Improving Paragraphs section, as it tends to be the easiest.

Sentence Corrections require you to determine if there is an error with the underlined portion of the sentence, and if so to pick the answer choice that corrects that error without creating new errors.

Below is a typical Sentence Correction question. Don't worry about working through the problem; you'll have a shot at that later. This example is here to familiarize you with the format.

1. Although he wrote over 2500 years ago, the Greek playwright Sophocles is still being <u>read, his plays</u> are performed on stages all over the world.

   (A) read, his plays are
   (B) read; his plays being
   (C) read: his plays are being
   (D) read; his plays are
   (E) read, yet his plays are

   Correct Answer: (D)

Error Ids require you to determine if one of the four underlined portions of the sentence contains an error. Always given is the option, (E) No Error.

14. <u>During</u> the 14th century, classical antiquity
       A
    gained renewed importance <u>when both</u> writers
                            B
    and artists <u>turned to</u> ancient Greek culture
               C
    <u>for</u> inspiration. <u>No error</u>
     D   E

    Correct Answer: (E)

The **Improving Paragraphs** section begins with an essay written by a student, and in the questions that follow, your job is to correct the student's errors.

Take a look at a sample passage and an Improving Paragraphs question on the next page. Don't worry about reading the passage or working through the question; I'm just providing a visual so you can easily notice when you are on the Improving Paragraphs section.

(1) Many parents consider video games violent and a waste of time and energy. (2) A recent version of the acclaimed video game Grand Theft Auto evoked disparaging reviews from child advocates, they are people who believe that violent games result in aggressive behavior in children and teens. (3) The only affirmative ones expressed relief that the Entertainment Software Rating Board (ESRB) rated the video game Mature. (4) Wouldn't they be forever scarred to play a video game that contained violence, strong language, and sexual content? (5) And Manhunt 2, the action/adventure game sequel to Rockstar Games 2003's Manhunt. (6) Imagine equating the violence one sees on the big screen with real life.

(7) I see nothing wrong with video games, whether violent or of the Guitar Hero variety. (8) After all, aren't Looney Tunes cartoons just as violent? (9) For example, remember the Bugs Bunny episode where Bugs pulls out a gun and shoots an innocent man for coughing? (10) Cartoons would never have become so popular if the gags did not include violence and innuendo. (11) No doubt, video game players recognize the violent actions of modern day video game characters, they are reminiscent of those of classic cartoon characters, such as Wile E. Coyote, created by the late Chuck Jones. (12) Jones will see traces of his characters in the antics of the Grand Theft Auto players. (13) Wile E. Coyote blows himself up with Acme Dynamite, and would feel right at home in the world of Grand Theft Auto.

(14) Violence has been prevalent in entertainment since the first cartoons, and we should not assume that children and teenagers are unable to differentiate violence for entertainment's sake, from real-life violence.

30. Which of the following is the best version of the underlined portion of sentence 2 (reproduced below)?

A recent version of the acclaimed video game Grand Theft Auto evoked disparaging reviews from child advocates, they are people who believe that violent games result in aggressive behavior in children and teens.

(A) (As it is now)
(B) child advocates; they were people who believed
(C) child advocates in believing
(D) child advocates. These believed
(E) child advocates, those who believe

Correct Answer: (E)

PROCESS OF ELIMINATION

Process of Elimination comes in handy on any standardized test. Often, the right answer is hidden among some very tempting wrong answers. The key is learning to spot and eliminate these wrong answers in order to increase your odds of choosing correctly. Every elimination increases your odds!

Remember: Messy tests are good tests. Statistics show that students who write on their exams, who ask rhetorical questions and physically eliminate answers, do better! So mark that test booklet up!

GUESSING

On multiple-choice questions you get ¼ of a point off for each wrong answer. On the Critical Reading and Math portions of the SAT, I tell you not to be afraid to leave answers blank, as you don't get penalized; however, I want you to take educated guesses on EVERY question on the Writing sections. I give you all the grammar rules you need to know, which means you should be able to eliminate AT LEAST two (probably more) answer choices. You should be taking educated guesses. If you are absolutely stuck on a question and can't eliminate ANY answer choices, then you are off the hook and can leave it blank, but after studying the grammar rules in this book, I doubt you will find yourself in that situation.

HOW TO USE THIS BOOK

I've structured this book so that you can skip around to different chapters if you already know your strengths and weaknesses. I encourage you to work through the whole book, but if you are a higher scoring student you might only need coaching on some of the trickier grammar rules.

Each chapter that covers the grammar rules contains a lecture on the different rules with sample problems illustrating each, and a comprehensive drill at the end. An answer key and explanation of the problems follow every comprehensive drill.

Before reviewing the material in this book or on the DVDs, take a PSAT or other SAT diagnostic test, such as a diagnostic test in *The Official SAT Study Guide*. A basic familiarity with the test and a baseline score to monitor your progress will provide a helpful frame of reference.

Let's start with the different question types and the best technique to use for each.

Chapter 1
The Technique

The *Sentence Correction* questions should be approached in an entirely different manner than the *Error ID* questions, but one thing holds true for both types:

⟶ **You cannot depend on your ear to lead you to the right answer.**

The mistake most students make is to judge an answer choice based on the way it SOUNDS. It SOUNDS wrong, so I don't want to pick it. Answer choice (B) SOUNDS better so I'll chose it. Sounding right is not legitimate justification for choosing an answer, and often an answer choice that sounds wrong is actually correct.

Here's why: People don't speak in a grammatically correct manner. What might sound right (because of the way we are used to hearing people talk) could totally violate a grammar rule. So rather than justifying an answer choice with "it sounds right" or eliminating an answer choice because "it sounds wrong," base your picks on one of the 19 grammar rules covered in Chapters 3-5.

Now I'm going to contradict myself; using your ear to test prepositions is oftentimes helpful, and you can get away with using your ear on the Sentence Corrections more than you can on the Error IDs. But trust me, picking an answer and justifying it with a grammar rule feels so much better than using that silly phrase, "it just sounds right."

Sentence Corrections Technique

There are 25 Sentence Correction problems on the SAT. ETS underlines either a portion of the sentence, or the entire sentence. There can be more than one error in the underlined portion of the sentence. The non-underlined portion of the sentence is ALWAYS correct and CANNOT be changed. Your job is to determine whether the underlined portion has errors, or is correct as written.

> **Answer Choice (A) is the underlined portion of the sentence as originally written, so if there is no error, then pick (A). If there is an error, then immediately eliminate (A). No need to look at it again.**

Step 1: Read the entire sentence and decide if there is an error.

Option #1: No Error

⟶ **If you believe the sentence is correct as written, you should still go through answer choices (B) through (E) to make sure you aren't missing something and that there is not a better option.**

Let's see how this works:

1. Geology is the study of the materials that make up the earth, <u>especially their compositions, structures, and reactions to processes that act upon them.</u>

   (A) especially their compositions, structures, and reactions to processes that act upon them
   (B) and especially they are concerned with their compositions, structures, and reactions to processes that act upon them
   (C) especially studying their compositions, structures, and reactions to processes that act upon them
   (D) especially their compositions, structures, and with their reactions to processes that act upon them
   (E) with special study of their compositions, structures, and including reactions to processes that act upon them

Follow Step 1 and read the sentence in its entirety. An error probably didn't pop out at you, but to be on the safe side, take a walk through answer choices (B) – (E).

(B)   notice how ETS has inserted an ambiguous "they" into the sentence. *Who* is "they"? Geologists? "Geologists" is never stated in the sentence, so the "they" is incorrect.

(C)   by inserting "studying" the sentence has become confusing and unnecessarily wordy. *Who* is studying? If anything "the study" is "studying" and that doesn't make any sense.

(D)   this answer choice is not parallel. We have *compositions* (a noun), *structures* (a noun) and then following the last comma ETS has inserted *and with their* before the noun *reactions*, throwing the parallel construction of the sentence all off.

(E)   why use the wordy and awkward *with special study*, when we can keep it simple and use *especially*. This answer choice is also not parallel. Inserting the verb "including" before the noun "reactions" messes up the parallel construction of *compositions* (noun), *structures* (noun), and *reactions* (noun).

Correct Answer: (A)

I realize that the justifications given above may seem foreign to you, but once we cover the grammar rules they should all make sense; for now, concentrate on the technique.

Option #2: Known Error

  ⟶ **If you read the sentence and know the error, immediately eliminate answer choice (A) and every other answer choice that contains that error.**

Let's try a problem like this together:

2. Traveling through Switzerland, <u>the scenery of snow-capped mountains and clear lakes, which I photographed, was stunning.</u>

   (A) the scenery of snow-capped mountains and clear lakes, which I photographed, was stunning
   (B) the snow-capped mountains and clear lakes were the stunning scenery I photographed
   (C) I photographed the stunning scenery of snow-capped mountains and clear lakes
   (D) I photographed the scenery of snow-capped mountains and clear lakes, being stunning
   (E) what I photographed was the stunning scenery of snow-capped mountains and clear lakes

The error might not have jumped out at you, but that's only because we haven't covered the grammar rules. So, let's say you noticed the **Misplaced Modifier** error the first time you read the sentence. The introductory phrase *Traveling through Switzerland* modifies the noun that directly follows: *the scenery*. Can the "scenery" be "traveling through Switzerland"? No! Who is really traveling through Switzerland? *I* am. So the "I" needs to directly follow the intro phrase "traveling through Switzerland." That means we can eliminate (A) and (B), which has *the snow-capped mountains and clear lakes* traveling through Switzerland, and (E) which has *what I photographed* traveling through Switzerland. That leaves us with (C) and (D) which correctly have "I" directly after the modifying phrase. *Traveling through Switzerland, I…*

Step 2: Compare the answers you have left.

In this case, (C) and (D).

     (C)   I like it. I can't find anything wrong with it.
     (D)   inserts a "being," and if there is one thing I want you to take from this book, it's that
             ⟶ ***"being" is bad.*** ⟵
             Don't pick an answer choice with "being" in it, especially when you have a perfectly good alternate answer without a "being" to choose from.

Correct Answer: (C)

Option #3: Unknown Error

⟶ **If you read the sentence and you have a hunch there is an error but just can't place it, skim through the answer choices to see if you can visually spot similarities and differences.**

This comparison will clue you in to the error, and ultimately help you save time. Check it out:

3. There is many challenges associated with living
with someone for the first time.

    (A) is many challenges associated
    (B) is many challenges to associate
    (C) is many challenges associating
    (D) are many challenges associated
    (E) are many challenges which associate

Let's assume you did NOT catch the **Subject Verb Agreement** error when you read the sentence. But you do believe there is an error. Skim the answer choices for a visual tip off. Notice that (A), (B), and (C) start with "is" and (D) and (E) start with "are." There's your error. Before reading the answer choices, ask: *What* "is" or "are"? *Challenges*. "Challenges" is plural, so it needs to be partnered with a plural verb, *are*. Eliminate (A), (B), and (C), which all have "is." No sense in wasting time reading them.

Step 2: Compare the answers you have left.

In this case, (D) and (E).

        (D)   "are many challenges associated…" fixes the error and doesn't create any new errors. I like it.
        (E)   "are many challenges" works but "which associate" changes the intended meaning of the sentence. Now instead of *challenges BEING associated with*, the *challenges are DOING the associating*.

Correct Answer: (D)

> **When you look at the answer choices for similarities and differences, don't just look at the beginning of the underlined phrase. The error might be in the middle and is very often at the end of the underlined portion of the sentence.**

One of those three approaches should be used on every Sentence Correction question.

Here are some additional tips to keep in mind when dealing with Sentence Corrections:

Beware of answers that fix an error, but create a new error!
    •   ETS loves to fix an error in an answer choice, but create a new one. Don't fall for it!

The shortest, most concise answers are the best!
    •   Stay away from wordy, long answer choices.

Beware of "ing" words, especially "having" and "being!"
    •   "ing" words are notorious for creating sentence fragments and wordy, confusing sentences.

Error ID Technique

Error IDs require a different technique. Four different parts of the given sentence are underlined. Either 1 of the 4 is wrong, or none of the 4 are wrong. Don't be afraid to pick (E) No Error. Approximately 1 out of 5 correct answers is (E) No Error. That does not mean I want you to count and make sure you are meeting the 1 out of 5 quota. Rather, if you are having trouble on an Error ID and can't seem to pinpoint an error, *don't hesitate to pick (E)!*

Step 1: Read the sentence in its entirety.

Students tend to "jump" at what they THINK is the right answer. Slow down. Do yourself a favor and read the ENTIRE sentence before you bubble in your answer. Sometimes when I read a sentence, what I think is an error is replaced by an even worse error later in the sentence. Had I picked my first instinct, I would never have seen the glaringly wrong answer choice that followed.

Step 2: Fix and Justify the Error.

You do not get to pick an answer as wrong UNLESS you can JUSTIFY the error with a grammar rule. Ideally you want to be able to FIX the error AND JUSTIFY.

Option #1: Known Error

If you read the sentence and you catch the error, terrific! Fix it and justify it to be absolutely certain you are correct.

Let's try one together:

1. According to the Centers for Disease Control
       A
   and Prevention, the prevalence of obesity

   has risen quite noticeable over the past 20 years.
      B   C   D
   No error
      E

You might not have caught the error, as you have yet to learn the grammar rules, but let's say you spotted the **Adjective/Adverb** error in answer choice (C). *Noticeable* is an adjective modifying the verb *has risen*. But adjectives don't modify verbs, adverbs do. Change "noticeable" to "noticeably" and justify it with the grammar rule Adjective/Adverb.

Here's what your test booklet should look like:

1. According to the Centers for Disease Control
       A
   and Prevention, the prevalence of obesity
                noticeably   *Adjective / Adverb*
   has risen quite ~~noticeable~~ over the past 20 years.
      B   Ⓒ   D
   No error
      E

Option #2: Unknown Error or No Error

If you read the sentence and don't catch an error right off, don't just pick (E) No error! You must go through every answer choice before you pick that (E)!

Let's see this at play:

2. Neither Mr. Hutchinson <u>nor</u> Mr. Randall
                              A
   <u>thinks</u> that playing as many video games as <u>his</u>
      B   C
   daughter Veronica does <u>will lead</u> to anything
                              D
   fruitful. <u>No error</u>
                  E

Many students will read this sentence and not catch an error. But if you work through the answers one by one, you are sure to spot it.

(A)   "nor" is a preposition that tell us to check and make sure it is partnered with "neither." Yes it is!

(B)   "thinks" is a simple present tense verb. We should check to make sure the verb agrees in number with its subject. Ask: *Who* or *what* "thinks"? *Neither*. "Neither" is singular and "thinks" is singular so that checks. The sentence is set in the present, so "thinks" is the correct verb tense as well.

(C)   "his" is a pronoun. The easiest rule to check for first is **Pronoun Ambiguity**. *Who* does the "his" refer to? Hmmm….we have two men in the sentence: *Mr. Hutchinson and Mr. Randall*, so we don't know to whom the "his" belongs. Is Veronica Mr. Hutchinson's daughter, or Mr. Randall's? We've caught our grammar rule! No need to go any further.

Here's what your test booklet should look like:

2. Neither Mr. Hutchinson <u>nor</u> Mr. Randall
                              A   Mr. Hutchinson's or Mr. Randall's   Pronoun Ambiguity
   <u>thinks</u> that playing as many video games as <u>his</u>
      B   Ⓒ
   daughter Veronica does <u>will lead</u> to anything
                              D
   fruitful. <u>No error</u>
                  E

The Drills that follow the Grammar Lessons are made up of both Sentence Correction and Error ID problems. A detailed explanation of each of the questions follows in the Answers and Explanations sections. I give explanations for every single answer choice (either what makes it wrong, or what makes it right). I don't necessarily go through the shortcuts the techniques provide. So remember to eliminate as you go, as often it won't be necessary to run through every answer choice.

The Improving Paragraphs technique I leave for the Improving Paragraphs Chapter, which is best reviewed AFTER learning all the grammar rules. Before we delve into the grammar rules, however, let's review some basic Parts of Speech in the next chapter.

Chapter 2
Parts of Speech

THE BASICS

Let's start with the basic parts of speech tested on the SAT: *Nouns, Pronouns, Verbs, Adjectives, Adverbs, Conjunctions,* and *Prepositions.* In this section, I am just skimming the surface. I will go much more in depth with exactly how these parts of speech are tested on the SAT when we discuss the specific grammar rules.

NOUNS: A noun is a person, place, thing, or idea.

Let's look at some examples of *concrete nouns* – nouns that you can experience with your five senses: sight, taste, touch, hearing, and smell.

Person – boy, president, teacher...
Place – laundry mat, mall, school...
Thing – ball, broccoli, dinosaur...

Abstract nouns are a bit more difficult to spot. You can't see them, hear them, taste them, touch them, or smell them.

Idea – happiness, love, warmth, politeness...

Singular versus Plural – ETS loves to test singular versus plural nouns.

A *singular noun* is one person, one place, one thing, or one idea – girl, gymnasium, ocean...

A *plural noun* is more than one person, place, thing, or idea – girls, gymnasiums, oceans...

> **To make a noun plural add an "s" on the end. The singular noun (boy) becomes the plural noun (boys).**

PRONOUNS: Pronouns are words that replace nouns.

Pronouns: he, her, we, I, they, it, whose, my, you, this, that, those, which…

Take a look at the following sentence: *Sally was nervous about Sally's first day of school, so Sally asked Sally's dad to drive slowly.*

With all those Sallys we have a tongue twister on our hands. We only need to say Sally once. The rest of the Sallys can be replaced by pronouns. ⟶ **Pronoun Alert!**

*Sally was nervous about **her** first day of school so **she** asked **her** dad to drive slowly.*

VERBS: A verb expresses an action, state of being, or occurrence.

There are three types of verbs to watch out for: action verbs, helping verbs, and state of being (linking) verbs.

Action: run, dance, pout…

State of Being:

is	are	am	was	were	be	being	been

Each of these 8 state of being verbs can also be used as helping verbs.

One can say, "I am sick" or "I am getting sick." In the second example, "am" is being used as a helping verb, lending a hand to the "getting."

Helping Verbs:

is	are	am	was	were	be	being	been	do	does	did	have	had
has	may	might	must	should	could	would	will	can	shall			

⟶ **Pay close attention to *have, has, had,* and *will*.**

These verbs are constantly tested on the SAT and the key to our verb tense rules.

ETS enjoys testing *singular versus plural verbs* as well.

⟶ **Singular verbs belong with singular nouns and plural verbs belong with plural nouns.**

Singular Verb: giggles, teaches, hikes…

Plural Verb: giggle, teach, hike…

> **The trick for verbs is opposite that of nouns. A singular verb has an "s" on the end, so to make a verb plural, remove the "s."**

You can always test singular versus plural with the nouns "girl" versus "girls."

*The girl **dances** versus The girls **dance**.*

14

ADJECTIVES: An adjective is a word that describes a noun.

Adjectives: beautiful, sad, interesting, orange…

Let's see some adjectives at play:

The *frisky* puppy
The *stylish* singer
The *timid* child

ADVERBS: Adverbs modify verbs, adjectives, and other adverbs.

> **Often, adverbs end in "ly."**

Adverbs: constantly, quickly, extremely, confidently…

Don't assume that just because a word ends in "ly" it is an adverb. Here are some common adjectives that end in "ly": *lovely, lonely, motherly, friendly, neighborly.*

Adverbs often tell WHEN something happens, WHERE something happens, HOW something happens, UNDER WHAT CONDITIONS something happens, or TO WHAT DEGREE something happens.

> *Adverb Alert!*

When: She arrived **early** for her date.
Where: The hummingbird made a nest **outside**.
How: Sore from his workout, he moved **slowly** down the stairs.
Degree: I am **too** tired to go for a run.

Adverbs modify verbs: The tiger ran rapidly.
> The adverb *rapidly* is modifying the verb *ran*, letting us know HOW.

Adverbs modify adjectives: He is an unusually bad cook.
> The adverb *unusually* modifies the adjective *bad*, letting us know TO WHAT DEGREE.

Adverbs modify other adverbs: The teacher ran out of patience very quickly.
> The adverb *very* modifies the adverb *quickly*, letting us know TO WHAT DEGREE.

CONJUNCTIONS: Conjunctions are words that connect parts of a sentence.

Conjunctions: and, but, or, yet, by, because, so, although, since, while...

I'll give you a more in depth list later, but just remember conjunctions are *direction* words. All you have to ask is,

⟶ **"Do I want to keep going the same direction, or switch?"**

Same direction: I really enjoy running **and** want to sign up for the marathon.
Opposite direction: I really hate cilantro, **but** I will eat it if it comes in the burrito.

PREPOSITIONS: Prepositions are linking words that connect nouns, pronouns, and phrases to other parts of a sentence.

Prepositions: with, for, to, on, beside, over, against, of...

> *Lou has no tolerance **for** loud children.*
> *It is difficult to distinguish Tyler Winklevoss **from** Cameron Winklevoss.*

I will give you a more comprehensive list of prepositions in the idiom section of this book. You should memorize all the prepositions; not knowing them will cost you points.

That's it for the basic parts of speech. You have the necessary foundation; now let's tackle the grammar rules!

Chapter 3
Verb Errors

This chapter deals with 3 of the biggest grammar rules tested on the SAT: *Subject Verb Agreement, Verb Tense,* and *Parallelism.*

Each of these grammar rules tests something to do with verbs, and together they account for roughly 40 to 50% of the errors on the grammar portion of the SAT. So know them and know them well! Here's something they all have in common: The way to spot these errors is to LOOK FOR UNDERLINED VERBS!

Let's deal with our first grammar rule: Subject Verb Agreement.

Rule #1: Subject Verb Agreement

How to Find: **Underlined verbs, especially simple past and present tense verbs.**

How to Fix: **Make the verb agree in number with the subject it refers to.**

Let's refer to Subject Verb Agreement as SVA from here on out.

We've already discussed SVA a bit: Singular verbs go with singular nouns, and plural verbs go with plural nouns. *She studies* versus *They study.* From here it gets a bit fancier.

SVA Trick #1

The following pronouns are ALWAYS SINGULAR:

each   either   neither   all the **ones** and all the **bodys**
(**one   someone   anyone   no one   everyone   somebody   anybody   nobody   everybody**)

→ **ETS likes to keep you from noticing these pronouns by separating them from the verb with a prepositional phrase.**

Put a line through all prep phrases!

Prep phrases are easy to spot: They begin with a preposition.

of the dogs…   **with** her mother…
by the water…   **about** the chemistry test…
in the restaurant….   **to** the store…

If you can get in the habit of crossing out all prep phrases you won't ever be tricked by SVA again. Why? Because, the subject of the verb will not be inside the prep phrase!

The subject of the sentence can NEVER be the object of the preposition.

Let's identify our parts of speech in the following sentence.

Sally gave the gift to me.

What is the subject? **Sally** (The subject is usually the person or thing that is performing the action.)
What is the verb? **gave** (It is the action that the subject (*Sally*) is doing.)
What is the Direct Object? **the gift** (The direct object is the primary object affected by the transitive verb that comes before it.)
What is the Indirect Object? **me** (The indirect object is the person for whom the verb is performed. *Me* is the indirect object that is receiving *the gift*. *Me* is the object of the preposition *to*.)

Let's see how this works with the singular pronouns mentioned:

Neither of the two teachers enjoys attending conferences on the weekend.

Let's eliminate the prep phrases "of the two teachers" and "on the weekend," because we don't want to get tricked and identify the wrong subject.

Neither ~~of the two teachers~~ enjoys attending conferences ~~on the weekend~~.

What is the verb? **enjoys attending**
What is the subject? **neither** (I know it's tempting to pick "teachers" as the subject, but it is inside the prep phrase and so cannot be the subject.)

Now we have to check to see if the subject and verb match. *Neither* is singular and *enjoys* (with an "s" on the end) is also singular, so the sentence is correct as is.

Each of the cheerleaders get a set of pom poms for free.

Let's eliminate the prep phrases "of the cheerleaders," "of pom poms," and "for free."

Each ~~of the cheerleaders~~ get a set ~~of pom poms for free~~.

What is the verb? **get**
What is the subject? **each**
Do the subject and verb match? <u>Nope</u>. "Each" is singular and "get" is plural so we need to turn "get" into "gets."

*Each of the cheerleaders **gets** a set of pom poms for free.*

18

SVA Trick #2

The following pronouns can be SINGULAR or PLURAL:

some	all	any	most	none

$\longrightarrow$ **When dealing with the aforementioned pronouns, we have to** *look inside the prep phrase to see what the pronoun is referring to.*

Let's see how this works:

Most of the records are obsolete.

Be sure to cross out the prep phrase "of the records."

Most ~~of the records~~ are obsolete.

What is the verb? **are**
What is the subject? **most**
Do they match? "Are" is plural and "most" can be singular or plural so let's look inside the prep phrase to see what the "most" refers to – *records*. "Records" is plural so the subject and verb match and the sentence is correct.

Notice how you can count records? Watch what happens when you cannot count what is inside the prep phrase.

All of the cake have been eaten.

Cross out "of the cake."

All ~~of the cake~~ have been eaten.

What is the verb? **have been eaten**
What is the subject? **all**
Do they match? Nope. Look inside the prep phrase and realize that "all" refers to "cake." "Cake" is singular – you can count *pieces of cake*, but you can't count *cake*. *Have been eaten* is plural so we need to change it to *has been eaten*.

All of the cake **has** *been eaten.*

SVA Trick #3

Here is our last set of tricky pronouns.

who, **which**, and **that** can be **SINGULAR or PLURAL**

19

With these guys, it's not as easy as checking inside the prep phrase to see what they refer to. Let's see if you can figure out the trick.

*Michelle is one of those girls who **is/are** always checking **her/their** makeup in the mirror.*

Circle your guess first!

Is the subject of the sentence "Michelle," "one," or "girls?" Technically the subject is "who" – *who is*. But "who" is a pronoun that can be singular or plural, so *what* does the "who" refer to – *Michelle, one*, or *girls*?

> **who, which,** and **that** refer to **whatever noun or pronoun is closest.**

girls is closest to *who*, so the "who" is plural. The sentence should read:

*Michelle is one of those girls who **are** always checking **their** makeup in the mirror.*

SVA Trick #4

Ever heard of *compound subjects?*

⟶ **Sometimes the same verb can refer to more than one subject.**

Sam and Mary race each other home every day.

"Race" is the verb and "Sam and Mary" is the compound subject.

> **Two subjects linked by "*and*" are plural.**

ETS won't make it that easy though. The sentence will be constructed more along the lines of: *In the kitchen cupboard there is a can of beans and two boxes of macaroni and cheese that expired 8 months ago.*

Let's cross out our prep phrases.

~~In the kitchen cupboard~~ there is a can ~~of beans~~ and two boxes ~~of macaroni and cheese~~ that expired 8 months ago.

What is the verb? **is**
What is the subject? **can** AND **two boxes** (We have a compound subject that is easy to miss due to all the prep phrases and the fact that the subject comes AFTER the verb instead of before.)
Do they match? Nope. Two subjects joined by "and" are plural. *Is* should be *are.*

*In the kitchen cupboard there **are** a can of beans and two boxes of macaroni and cheese that expired 8 months ago.*

> **Whenever you see "there is" or "there are" always look after to find the subject.**

What about two subjects linked by "or" or "nor"?

Take a look at the following example. Circle your answer.

*Neither the customers nor the saleslady **like/likes** the black dress.*

We have two subjects: *customers* and *saleslady*, but the correct subject of the verb is "saleslady" (because it is the closest noun to the verb) so the sentence should read:

*Neither the customers nor the saleslady **likes** the black dress.*

If I flipped the order of "customers" and "saleslady" then the correct choice would be the plural "like."

*Neither the saleslady nor the customers **like** the black dress.*

> **When two subjects are linked by "or" or "nor," the verb agrees with the subject closest to it.**

SVA Trick #5

⟶ *Collective Nouns* **are nouns that indicate or specify a group of people or things, but are thought of as a singular unit.**

Collective nouns: government, herd, team, society, army, audience, family…

There is more than one soldier in an army, but "army" is a singular subject.

> **Countries are always singular: The United States, The Philippines, France…**

That's a lot of information for just one grammar rule, but it's one of the most commonly tested errors on the SAT. Not all 18 grammar rules will be so loaded.

Rule #2: Verb Tense

How to Find: **Underlined Verbs, especially when combined with the helping verbs "had," "has," and "have."**

How to Fix: **Change to the correct verb form.**

This grammar rule is a biggie. Let's start with some verb terminology.

The Infinitive: the form of the verb that is not conjugated. It will usually have a "to" in front of it – *to study, to dance, to work…*

Gerund: The verb conjugated in the "ing" form and used as a noun – *studying, dancing, working…*

Past Participle: The verb conjugated in the "ed" form – *studied, danced, worked…*

> **When the past participle is used without a helping verb (studied) it denotes an action in the past that has been completed, but if the past participle is partnered with a helping verb (has studied) it does not denote the simple past, but one of the trickier tenses.**

There are 6 verb tenses you need to know for the SAT. Let's tackle the easy ones first: *present*, *past*, and *future*.

#1: Present Tense

Present tense is used when an action occurs in THE PRESENT time.

There are two types of present tenses ETS will test: *simple present* and *present progressive*.

Simple Present: Indicates actions that are habitual or always true.
- *John **studies** at the library everyday.*
- *I **like** ice cream.*
- *Susie **goes** to church.*

Simple present can also be used to refer to actions that are to occur at a specific time in the future.
- *Bob **works** at 9 am.*

> **Simple present is typically formed with the infinitive without the "to" combined with an "s" on the end for 3rd person singular.**

Example: I **run**
            He **runs**
            She **runs**
            They **run**
            We **run**

Present Progressive: Indicates actions that are temporary and are occurring now.
- *Ryan **is wondering** what he scored on the test.*
- *Luke **is taking** a break from college this semester.*
- *She **is working** at a café right now.*

Present Progressive can also be used to specify an action that will occur in the near future.
- *She **is getting married** on Saturday.*
- *I **am going** to the grocery store in the morning.*

> **Present Progressive is formed with a "to be" verb plus a gerund (ing) word.**

Example: I **am running**
He **is running**
She **is running**
They **are running**
We **are running**

ETS typically won't test the differences between simple present and present progressive (meaning they won't give you the present progressive and expect you to change it to simple present - unless of course the two verb forms are not parallel) so keep it simple:

⟶ **just know that these two present tense verb forms occur in the present time and should not be confused with any of the past tenses, future tenses, or the present perfect tense.**

#2: Past Tense

Past tense is used when an action occurs before the present time, or in the PAST.

There are two types of easy past tenses ETS will test: *simple past* and *past progressive*.

Simple Past: Indicates an action that happened at a specific time in the past and is completed.
- *I **studied** in China last year.*
- *Lou **washed** his car on Saturday.*
- *He **did not adopt** the puppy.* (Notice I did not list a specific time, but there is an implied specific time and that is all we need.)

Simple past can also be used to indicate a habitual action in the past.
- *He **never helped** his father wash the dishes.*
- *Debbie **always cried** when her mother left for work.*

> **Simple Past is typically formed with an "ed" on the end of the verb.**

Example: I *talked*
He *talked*
She *talked*
They *talked*
We *talked*

Past Progressive: Indicates an action that is interrupted by another action in the past.
- *I **was playing** tennis when I got the phone call.*
- *I **was sleeping** soundly, while Mike played video games in the living room.*
- *When she arrived, we **were baking** a cake.* (Notice how the verb that is being interrupted (were baking) is conjugated in the past progressive form and the verb that is doing the interrupting (arrived) is conjugated in the simple past form.)

Past Progressive can also indicate an action that is interrupted by a specific time in the past. (Not an action that started or stopped in the past - that is simple past - but an action that is INTERRUPTED!)

- *Yesterday at 8 pm, I **was watching** a movie.* (Translation: I started watching a movie earlier than 8, and was still watching the movie at 8 – therefore, *Past Progressive*.)
- *Yesterday at 8 pm, I **watched** a movie.* (Translation: I started watching the movie AT 8 - therefore, *Simple Past*.)

Past Progressive is formed with a "to be" verb plus a gerund (ing) word.

Example: I **was talking**
                You **were talking**
                She **was talking**
                He **was talking**
                They **were talking**
                We **were talking**

ETS typically won't test the differences between simple past and past progressive (meaning they won't give you the past progressive and expect you to change it to simple past - unless of course the two verb forms are not parallel), so keep it simple:

$\longrightarrow$ **just know that these two past tense verb forms occur in the PAST and should not be confused with any of the trickier past tenses, future tenses, or present tenses.**

#3: Future Tense

Future Tense is used when a specific action occurs in the FUTURE.

The two types of easy future tenses ETS tests are the simple future and future progressive.

Simple Future: Indicates a voluntary action (*I will lend you my dress*), a prediction (*Tomorrow, it will snow*), or a specific planned action (*I will study for the test tomorrow night*).

The simple future is partnered with the simple present when introduced by **when, as soon as, until, after, before,** and **while**.

- ***When*** *the bell rings, we **will go play** on the playground.*
- *They **will go** to the mall **as soon as** they get their paycheck.*

The future tense is formed with "will" or "shall" plus the infinitive form of the verb.

Example: I **will dance**
                You **will dance**
                He **will dance**
                She **will dance**
                They **will dance**
                We **will dance**

Future Progressive: Like the past progressive, the future progressive indicates an action that is interrupted by another action in the future.

- *I **will be sleeping** when he returns.*
- *When she arrives, we **will be baking** a cake.* (Notice how the verb that is being interrupted is conjugated in the future progressive form (will be baking) and the verb that is doing the interrupting (arrives) is conjugated in the simple present form.)

Future Progressive can also indicate an action that is interrupted by a specific time in the future. (Not an action that starts or stops in the future - that is simple future -but an action that is INTERUPPTED!)

- *Tomorrow at 8 pm, I **am going to be watching** a movie.* (Translation: I am going to start watching a movie earlier than 8, and will still be watching the movie at 8.)
- *Tomorrow at 8pm, I **will watch** a movie.* (Translation: I am going to start watching the movie AT 8.)

The future progressive is formed with "will" plus "be" plus a gerund (ing) word.

Example: I **will be waiting**
You **will be waiting**
He **will be waiting**
She **will be waiting**
They **will be waiting**
We **will be waiting**

ETS will not expect you to differentiate the different uses of simple future and future progressive, so keep it simple:

⟶ **just remember that whatever form you see it in, the future tense happens in the future!**

Moving on to the trickier tenses: *Present Perfect, Past Perfect, Future Perfect*, and *Subjunctive*. The key to getting verb tense issues correct is learning how to spot the error in the first place!

#4: Present Perfect

How to Find: "has" or "have" plus the past participle – *have seen, has run, have begun, has sung...*

Example: I **have run**
You **have run**
He **has run**
She **has run**
They **have run**
We **have run**

> **"Has" or "have" used alone is just simple present tense, so if you see it connected to a past participle such as "eaten," "finished," or "rung" you know you are dealing with the present perfect.**

Oftentimes, ETS will trick us because they will use present perfect correctly, but will combine it with the wrong past participle.

Take a look at the following example:

*He **rang** the doorbell.*
- In this instance, "rang" is a simple past tense verb.

*He **has rung** the doorbell often.*
- In this instance, "has rung" is present perfect.
- ETS might write this instead – *He **has rang** the doorbell often* – although present perfect tense is correct, it is combined with the simple past, not the past participle, so *rang* should be *rung*.

ALWAYS GO WITH THE "U" FORM OF THE VERB WHEN COMBINED WITH A HELPING VERB LIKE "HAS" OR "HAVE"!

> **Don't be thrown if you see present perfect conjugated as "has been eating" or "have been eating." It's still the present perfect and the rules still apply.**

Present Perfect Usage #1: **Indicates an action or experience from the past that occurred at no set time and may have happened more than once.**
- *He **has lived** in Sweden.*
- *She **has traveled** to Europe.*
- *I **have seen** an elephant.*
- *She **has studied** here often.*
- *They **have played** together five times over the last few months.*

Let's take a look at the following example:

*She **has traveled** to Europe.*
- As written, this sentence indicates that at some point between the past and present she has been to Europe versus...

*I **traveled** to Europe 2 years ago.*
- As written, this sentence indicates a specific time in the past (2 years ago), so simple past tense (traveled) is correct.

Present Perfect Usage #2: **Indicates a change that has occurred.**

- *I **have bought** a car.*
- *She **has grown** into a beautiful lady.*
- ***Has** the sweater **gone** on sale?*

Present Perfect Verb!

Let's pick apart the following example:

*She **has grown** into a beautiful lady.*

As written, this sentence indicates that somewhere between the past and the present she has grown from a child into a beautiful lady, signaling a change in occurrence.

Present Perfect Usage #3: **Indicates an action that started in the past and continues on into the present.**

- ***Ever since** she started dating Billy, she **has acted** like a prima donna.*
- *With their feet **still** in the water, they exclaimed, "we **have been playing** in the pond."*
- *"How long **have you been** friends with Tasha?"*

Let's analyze the following sentence:

***Ever since** she started dating Billy, she **has acted** like a prima donna.*

Notice the tip off of the chronological phrase *Ever since*. As written, the sentence indicates that she started acting like a prima donna as soon as she started dating Billy (sometime in the past) and she is still to this day acting like a prima donna.

> *since, ever since, ago, still,* **and** *over* **(as in:** *over the past two weeks*)
> **are clue words that present perfect is needed!**

#5: Past Perfect

How to Find: **"had" plus the past participle –** *had run, had begun, had eaten, had sung*…(notice those "u" forms – don't let them trick you and get away with "had began").

Example: I **had sung**
You **had sung**
He **had sung**
She **had sung**
They **had sung**
We **had sung**

> **"Had" used alone is simple past** - *He had a dog* - **versus present perfect**
> *He had adopted a dog, before he got sick.*

Don't be thrown if you see past perfect conjugated as "had been eating." It's still the past perfect and the rules still apply.

Past Perfect Usage: **Indicates an action in the past that occurs before a second action and is completed.**
- She **had made** the bed, before she went to school.
- They walked the dog after they **had given** it its doggy treats.
- By the time the principal quit, the school **had gone** to ruin.

---

before, *after*, *until*, and *by the time* are all clue words that the past perfect is needed.

Let's pick apart the following sentence:

They walked the dog after they had given it its doggy treats.

First notice the "had given" - we have past perfect tense on our hands.

Past perfect must have two actions in the sentence, so ask: *does the sentence have two past actions?*
Yes - "walked" and "had given."

Now ask, *does one action happen before the other?* Yes - they *walked the dog* AFTER they *gave the treats*.

The action that happens first in time belongs with the "had."

- They gave the treats first so it should be "had given."
- The action that happens second (walked) is always conjugated in the simple past.

#6: Future Perfect

How to Find: **"will have" plus the past participle.** – *will have run, will have begun, will have eaten, will have sung*…(notice those "u" forms – don't let them trick you and get away with "will have sang").

Example: I **will have** sung
You **will have** sung
He **will have** sung
She **will have** sung
They **will have** sung
We **will have** sung

The insertion of the "have" differentiates the future perfect from the simple perfect.

Future Perfect Usage: **Indicates an action in the future that occurs before a second action or event in the future.**

- She **will have bought** a dress by the time she gets married.
- I **will have arrived** at school by 9 am.
- They **will have cleaned** enough houses to buy a car before their in-laws come to town.

> **Words that indicate time, such as *before* and *by the time*, are clues that the future perfect is needed.**

Let's pick apart the following sentence:

She will have found an apartment by the time she moves.

First notice the "will have found" - we have a future perfect verb.

Future perfect must have two actions in the sentence (or a future action and a future event), so ask: *does the sentence have two future actions?* Yes – "will have found" and "moves."

Now ask, *does one action happen before the other?* Yes – she is *finding the apartment* BY THE TIME (meaning BEFORE) she *moves*.

> **The action that happens first in time belongs with the "will have."**

- She is going to find an apartment first so it should be "will have found."
- The action that happens second (moves) is always conjugated in the simple present.

Let's see how the future perfect works with a future action linked to a future event:

*By August 15th, I **will have finished** the summer program.*

The event (August 15th) contains an implied action: By (the time the date becomes) August 15th, I will have finished the summer program.

Verb Tense Tip: The best way to deal with verb tense is to set yourself up in time. Ask: *am I in the present, past, or future?* If you are in the present, you have two tenses to choose from, if in the past, three tenses, and if you are in the future, you have 2 tenses.

PRESENT	**PAST**	**FUTURE**
simple/progressive present	simple/progressive past	simple/progressive future
present perfect	present perfect	future perfect
	past perfect	

Subjunctive

Subjunctive Usage #1: Subjunctive is used when expressing urgency, or demanding or suggesting something.

The following words should always be followed by the subjunctive:

> To demand (that)
> To insist (that)
> To command (that)
> To mandate (that)
> To desire (that)
> To ask (that)
> To request (that)
> To urge (that)
> To suggest (that)
> To recommend (that)
> To advise (that)

Below are some examples of phrases that likewise require the subjunctive:

> It is essential (that)
> It is crucial (that)
> It is imperative (that)
> It is recommended (that)
> It is vital (that)
> It is a good idea (that)…

A sentence using the subjunctive is formed with a **subject #1**, followed by a **verb #1**, followed by a **"that"** followed by a **subject #2**, followed by a **verb #2**, with lots of stuff in the middle.

Check it out:

*Rick **demanded that Danica pay** him the money.*

The subject #1 is always performing the action (in this case Rick).
The verb #1 is always the urgency verb (in this case *demanded*).
The subject #2 is always the direct or receiving object (in this case *Danica* is receiving *the demand*).
The verb #2 is always the subjunctive (in this case *pay*).

> **The subjunctive is constructed as the infinitive without the "to." ("to pay" is written as "pay.")**

Let's do some more.

*The teacher **suggested that the students study** every night throughout the week rather than cramming for the test the night before.*

An easy check to see if subjunctive is being used properly is to stick a "to" in front of the second verb and see if it forms an infinitive: "to study" – yes! So the subjunctive is formed correctly.

Let's try another:

*It is essential that she **be** full when taking her medicine.*

We have our subjunctive tip off "it is essential" and we have a "that" and we have a second subject "she" so let's check our second verb (the subjunctive). Stick a "to" before the "be" – "to be full" – great! In this example, "be" is an infinitive without the "to."

Subjunctive Usage #2: There is a second application of the subjunctive that is used to indicate a prediction, hypothetical, or wish.

***If I were** a rich girl, **then I would have** all the money in the world.*

This type of subjunctive use comes into play with "if...then" phrases.
- The "if" phrase requires a "were." (If I *were* a rich girl...)
- The "then" phrase requires a "would" followed by the infinitive without the "to." (then I *would have*...)
- Let's check the "have" in this example. "To have" – that's the infinitive so "would have" works!

Sometimes the "then" is implied, not stated.

So we could rewrite the sentence: *If I were a rich girl, I would have all the money in the world.*

I could also flip-flop the "if...then" phrases: *I would have all the money in the world if I were a rich girl.*

OR I could leave the "if" out too: *Were I a rich girl, I would have all the money in the world!*

Let's do one more:

***If I were to move** to Hawaii, **I would live** in Maui.*

Is there a "were" in the "if" phrase? Yes!
- notice how the "were" in this sentence is followed by the infinitive "to move." If a verb follows the "were" it must be in infinitive form. So if ETS had - "If I were moving to Hawaii..." that would be incorrect.

Is there a "would" in the implied "then" phrase? Yes! (I would live...).

Is the subjunctive in the infinitive without the "to" form? Yes! "To live."

Here's how the subjunctive works when expressing a wish:

I wish she **were** *able to sing better* NOT *I wish she* **was** *able to sing better.*

Rule #3: Parallelism

How to Find: **A comma series (Andy** *hates to shop, clean, and cook***) or linking words.**

How to Fix: **Put the verb or noun into the correct form so that the phrases (or words) of the sentence are parallel (the same).**

Let's see how it works with a comma series:

Carol is well aware that if she wants to be a veterinarian she will need to go to college, study hard, and being thick-skinned.

Identify your comma series and underline the verb forms as written:

Carol is well aware that if she wants to be a veterinarian she will need to <u>go</u> to college, <u>study</u> hard, and <u>being</u> thick-skinned.

- *"being"* is NOT PARALLEL to *"go"* and *"study."* Change to *"be."*

Revised sentence: *Carol is well aware that if she wants to be a veterinarian she will need to go to college, study hard, and* **be** *thick-skinned.*

> **The parallelism issue could also be fixed by applying the "to" to EACH of the verbs – "...to go to college, to study hard, and to be thick-skinned."**

Let's take a little detour from parallelism to talk about the word BEING.

Repeat after me: **BEING is BAD.** You should probably NOT pick an answer choice that contains the word being unless the sentence reads "human being" or it needs to match another phrase in the sentence.

For instance: *The student was being mature while the professor was being childish.*
- In this case you need the second *being* to match the first and vice versa.

⟶ **Other than that - eliminate answer choices with** *being* **in them!**

Let's try one more comma series example.

The teacher was encouraged to grade her papers quickly, meticulously, and in a fair manner.

Identify your comma series and underline the words that need to be parallel:

The teacher was encouraged to grade her papers <u>quickly</u>, <u>meticulously</u>, and <u>in a fair manner</u>.

- *in a fair manner* is NOT PARALLEL to the adverbs *quickly* and *meticulously*. Change to *fairly*.

Revise to a parallel sentence: *The teacher was encouraged to grade her papers quickly, meticulously, and* **fairly**.

Below is a list of common linking words that often indicate a parallelism error might be lurking.

than	and	but	not only….but also	both…and	whether….or	either…or

Let's see these hint words at play:

A basketball player must be able to dribble the ball and shooting a basket.

Let's analyze the sentence:

A basketball player must be able <u>to dribble</u> the ball (and) <u>shooting</u> a basket.

"To dribble" is the infinitive form of the verb and "shooting" is the gerund form of the verb. That's not parallel! Change *shooting* to *to shoot* to fix.

Revised sentence: *A basketball player must be able* **to dribble** *the ball and* **to shoot** *a basket.*

⟶ **Whenever you see a gerund underlined all you need to ask is, "should it be an infinitive instead?" Likewise, when an infinitive is underlined ask, "should it be a gerund instead?" We'll refer to this as the Gerund/Infinitive Switch.**

Here's another one:

The MBA candidate was applying not only to Harvard, but also Stanford.

Can you spot the error?

The MBA candidate was applying not only to Harvard, but also **to** *Stanford.*

- there is a "to" after the "not only" so make sure that everything that follows the "but also" is in the EXACT same form.

Phew! That's it for verbs! Let's apply what you have learned to the following drill of Sentence Correction and Error ID problems. The questions are testing SVA, Verb Tense, or Parallelism.

Verb Drill

1. The suggestions for meditation techniques, spiritual practices, and balanced living found in the Yoga Sutras is helpful for yoga practitioners when they try to go beyond the physical postures for a deeper understanding of the ancient practice.

   (A) is helpful for yoga practitioners when they try to go beyond the physical postures
   (B) for yoga practitioners trying to go beyond the physical postures, is helpful
   (C) and which is helpful for yoga practitioners who try to go beyond the physical postures
   (D) are helpful for yoga practitioners trying to go beyond the physical postures
   (E) are those that are helpful and try to go beyond the physical postures

2. In developing a treatment plan for a patient, a doctor must look at medical history, test results, overall health, and different dietary needs at each stage of healing.

   (A) different dietary needs at each stage of healing
   (B) different stages of healing determining different dietary needs
   (C) healing at different stages determining different dietary needs
   (D) dietary needs at each different stage of healing
   (E) determining different dietary needs at each stage of healing

3. Although chewing gum while carrying on a conversation was once considered rude, teenagers have now found that to chew the same flavor gum when you converse makes it easier for many young people to relate and connect.

   (A) to chew the same flavor gum when you converse makes it easier for many young people to relate and connect
   (B) relating, as well as connecting, are easier for many young people when chewing the same flavor gum while conversing
   (C) chewing the same flavor gum during conversation makes relating and connecting easier for many young people
   (D) for the ease of many young people during conversation one should chew the same flavor gum to relate and connect
   (E) to make relating and connecting easier for many young people during conversations you should use chewing the same flavor gum

4. Frederick Douglass, the abolitionist leader, was an opponent of slavery, a supporter of social reform, and a master of political oratory.

   (A) was an opponent of slavery, a supporter of social reform, and a master of
   (B) was an opponent of slavery, a supporter of social reform, and he mastered
   (C) was an opponent of slavery, a supporter of social reform, and mastering
   (D) was an opponent of slavery, supported social reform, and a master of
   (E) opposed slavery, was a supporter of social reform, mastering

5. Fire code precautions aimed at reducing the likelihood of a fire <u>requires contractors to follow</u> fire safety measures for new buildings and structures that are already standing.

(A) requires contractors to follow
(B) require contractors following
(C) require contractors to follow
(D) that requires contractors to follow
(E) that require contractors following

6. The manager's demand that employees follow health code requirements and wash their hands after using the restroom <u>was not dogmatic but a wish</u> to keep both employees and customers healthy.

(A) was not dogmatic but a wish
(B) was not dogmatic but wished
(C) was not because he was dogmatic, he wished
(D) resulted not from dogmatism, but from a wish
(E) resulted not from dogmatism, but he wished

7. Almost 20 years after Elvis Presley won his third

Grammy <u>for</u> his <u>inspirational</u> performance of the
      A   B

gospel song *How Great Thou Art*, the nation

<u>distributing</u> a postage stamp to pay tribute to <u>him</u>.
      C   D
<u>No error</u>
      E

8. Before women began working in munitions factories

during World War II, the best way for women <u>to earn</u>
                                              A

a living in <u>both</u> England and America <u>has been</u> on the
            B   C

the domestic front with labor <u>regarded as</u> "women's
                                    D

work." <u>No error</u>
            E

9. <u>Among</u> the most dangerous complications that
      A

women face during pregnancy <u>are</u> "ectopic
                              B

pregnancy," the dangerous and <u>sometimes deadly</u>
                                    C

occurrence resulting from the improper <u>implantation of</u>
                                              D

the egg somewhere other than the womb. <u>No error</u>
                                              E

10. There <u>are</u> a long <u>but</u> concise list of major renovations
            A   B

to the new house that <u>resulted from</u> the mismanaged
                            C

<u>efforts of</u> the first contractor. <u>No error</u>
      D   E

11. <u>When Anna Webb began</u> to speak out against
            A

polygamy – she shared her husband, Mormon leader

Brigham Young, <u>with twenty-six other wives</u> – she
                        B

<u>had been</u> the first woman <u>to rebel</u> against the Mormon
      C   D

practice. <u>No error</u>
                E

12. The area <u>surrounded by</u> the Dodecanese islands to
                    A

the south, the Cyclades and Sporades islands to the

west, and a series of Greek and Turkish islands along

the Turkish coast <u>comprise</u> the islands <u>collectively</u>
                        B   C
<u>known as</u> the Northeast Aegean islands. <u>No error</u>
      D   E

13. Because the wind was <u>unusually strong</u>, Caroline
$\qquad\qquad\qquad\qquad$ A

$\qquad$ finished ten seconds behind her opponent <u>in</u> the relay
$\qquad\qquad\qquad\qquad\qquad\qquad\qquad\qquad$ B

$\qquad$ race, even though she had <u>ran steadily</u> all the way
$\qquad\qquad\qquad\qquad\qquad\qquad$ C

$\qquad$ <u>from</u> the starting line. <u>No error</u>
$\qquad$ D $\qquad\qquad\qquad\qquad$ E

14. The exercise ball used by physical fitness trainers <u>are</u>
$\qquad\qquad\qquad\qquad\qquad\qquad\qquad\qquad\qquad$ A

$\qquad$ very effective <u>in activating</u> the electromyographic
$\qquad\qquad\qquad\qquad$ B

$\qquad$ activity of the abdominal muscles, <u>thereby</u> making
$\qquad\qquad\qquad\qquad\qquad\qquad\qquad\qquad$ C

$\qquad$ core training <u>during exercise</u> more efficient. <u>No error</u>
$\qquad\qquad\qquad\qquad$ D $\qquad\qquad\qquad\qquad$ E

15. To demand that others do whatever <u>one</u> <u>wants them</u> to
$\qquad\qquad\qquad\qquad\qquad\qquad\qquad$ A $\qquad$ B

$\qquad$ do is often <u>ignoring</u> the wishes and <u>even</u> the needs of
$\qquad\qquad\qquad$ C $\qquad\qquad\qquad\qquad$ D

$\qquad$ those who care the most. <u>No error</u>
$\qquad\qquad\qquad\qquad\qquad\qquad$ E

Answers and Explanations

Answer Key:

1. (D)	**6.** (D)	**11.** (C)
2. (A)	**7.** (C)	**12.** (B)
3. (C)	**8.** (C)	**13.** (C)
4. (A)	**9.** (B)	**14.** (A)
5. (C)	**10.** (A)	**15.** (C)

1. The suggestions for meditation techniques, spiritual practices, and balanced living found in the Yoga Sutras <u>is helpful for yoga practitioners when they try to go beyond the physical postures</u> for a deeper understanding of the ancient practice.

   (A) is helpful for yoga practitioners when they try to go beyond the physical postures
   (B) for yoga practitioners trying to go beyond the physical postures, is helpful
   (C) and which is helpful for yoga practitioners who try to go beyond the physical postures
   (D) are helpful for yoga practitioners trying to go beyond the physical postures
   (E) are those that are helpful and try to go beyond the physical postures

Notice how some of the answer choices have "is" and some have "are." ETS is testing **SVA.** Be sure to cross out the prep phrases *for meditation techniques, spiritual practices, and balanced living* and *in the Yoga Sutras.* Then ask: *what* "is helpful"? *The suggestions.* "Suggestions" is plural and "is" is singular. *Is* should be *are.*

   (B)   "is" needs to be "are."
   (C)   "and which" creates a sentence fragment issue and "is" needs to be "are."
   (D)   we have an "are"!
   (E)   changes the meaning of the sentence indicating that the *suggestions* are trying to go beyond the physical postures, rather than the *practitioners* trying to go beyond the physical practices.

Revised Sentence:
The suggestions for meditation techniques, spiritual practices, and balanced living found in the Yoga Sutras <u>are helpful for yoga practitioners trying to go beyond the physical postures</u> for a deeper understanding of the ancient practice.

Correct Answer: (D)

2. In developing a treatment plan for a patient, a doctor must look at medical history, test results, overall health, and <u>different dietary needs at each stage of healing.</u>

    (A) different dietary needs at each stage of healing
    (B) different stages of healing determining different dietary needs
    (C) healing at different stages determining different dietary needs
    (D) dietary needs at each different stage of healing
    (E) determining different dietary needs at each stage of healing

Check out the comma series. ETS must be testing **Parallelism**. "Medical history" - we have an adjective/noun combo. After the second comma we have "test results" another adjective/noun combo. "Overall health" (adjective/noun) and "different dietary needs" (still follows the adjective/noun combo). Everything is parallel.

    (B)   "different stages" is parallel (adjective/noun combo), but the sentence is wordy and changes the intended meaning of the sentence. The doctor doesn't need to look at *different stages*; he needs to look at *dietary needs*.
    (C)   changes the intended meaning of the sentence. The doctor is not looking at *healing* he is looking at *dietary needs*.
    (D)   Inserting the "different" before "stage of healing" is wordy and unnecessary.
    (E)   "determining" is a verb, not a noun, so the sentence is no longer parallel.

Correct Answer: (A)

3. Although chewing gum while carrying on a conversation was once considered rude, teenagers have now found that <u>to chew the same flavor gum when you converse makes it easier for many young people to relate and connect.</u>

    (A) to chew the same flavor gum when you converse makes it easier for many young people to relate and connect
    (B) relating, as well as connecting, are easier for many young people when chewing the same flavor gum while conversing
    (C) chewing the same flavor gum during conversation makes relating and connecting easier for many young people
    (D) for the ease of many young people during conversation one should chew the same flavor gum to relate and connect
    (E) to make relating and connecting easier for many young people during conversations you should use chewing the same flavor gum

Notice the switch from the gerunds "chewing" and "carrying" to the infinitive "to chew." Something is not quite parallel. *To chew* needs to be *chewing* to fix the **Parallelism** error. ETS has also thrown in an "it," which we like to avoid whenever possible.

(B) "relating" looks good, and "connecting" looks good, but the sentence should read *relating IS* not *relating ARE*. ETS added a SVA error.

(C) *chewing, relating, connecting* – I'd say we are all parallel!

(D) where is the "one" all of a sudden coming from? This option is way wordy and also seems to affect the meaning of the sentence.

(E) This option is wordy and confusing. Why insert a "you"? And how do you *USE chewing?*

Revised Sentence:
Although chewing gum while carrying on a conversation was once considered rude, teenagers have now found that <u>chewing the same flavor gum during conversation makes relating and connecting easier for many young people.</u>

Correct Answer: (C)

4. Frederick Douglass, the abolitionist leader, <u>was an opponent of slavery, a supporter of social reform, and a master of</u> political oratory.

(A) was an opponent of slavery, a supporter of social reform, and a master of

(B) was an opponent of slavery, a supporter of social reform, and he mastered

(C) was an opponent of slavery, a supporter of social reform, and mastering

(D) was an opponent of slavery, supported social reform, and a master of

(E) opposed slavery, was a supporter of social reform, mastering

The sentence is correct as written, (an opponent, a supporter, and a master) but the comma series and the other answer choices should clue you in to the fact that ETS is testing **Parallelism**.

(B) *he mastered* (mastered is a verb) is not parallel to *an opponent of slavery* and *a supporter of social reform*. (Opponent and supporter are both nouns.)

(C) *mastering* (verb) is not parallel to *an opponent* and *a supporter* (nouns).

(D) *supported social reform* (supported is a verb) is not parallel to *an opponent* and *a master*. (Opponent and master are nouns.)

(E) *was a supporter of social reform* is wordy; *supported social reform* is the better option. *Mastering* creates a dependent clause and thus a Sentence Fragment error, and changes the meaning of the sentence.

Correct Answer: (A)

5. Fire code precautions aimed at reducing the likelihood of a fire <u>requires contractors to follow</u> fire safety measures for new buildings and structures that are already standing.

(A) requires contractors to follow
(B) require contractors following
(C) require contractors to follow
(D) that requires contractors to follow
(E) that require contractors following

Notice the shift in the answer choices from "requires" to "require." ETS is testing **SVA**. *Who* or *what* "requires"? Cross out the prep phrase *at reducing the likelihood of a fire*. "Precautions" is plural and "requires" is singular, so we have an SVA error.

(B)   "require" is correct because it is plural, but the gerund "following" creates a sentence fragment error.

(C)   "require" is correct as is the infinitive "to follow."

(D)   The pronoun "that" refers to "fire" and indicates that the *FIRE* is requiring the *contractors to follow*, instead of the *PRECAUTIONS requiring*. The insertion of the "that" also creates a sentence fragment error.

(E)   The pronoun "that" refers to "fire" and indicates that the *FIRE* is requiring the *contractors to follow*, instead of the *PRECAUTIONS requiring*. The insertion of the "that" also creates a sentence fragment error. "Fire" is singular and "require" is plural so we also have a SVA error.

Revised Sentence:
Fire code precautions aimed at reducing the likelihood of a fire <u>require contractors to follow</u> fire safety measures for new buildings and structures that are already standing.

Correct Answer: (C)

6. The manager's demand that employees follow
   health code requirements and wash their hands after
   using the restroom <u>was not dogmatic but a wish</u> to
   keep both employees and customers healthy.

   (A) was not dogmatic but a wish
   (B) was not dogmatic but wished
   (C) was not because he was dogmatic, he wished
   (D) resulted not from dogmatism, but from a wish
   (E) resulted not from dogmatism, but he wished

Notice the tip-off word "but" and spot the **Parallelism** error. "dogmatic" is an adjective and "wish" is a noun. They are not parallel.

(B)	"dogmatic" is an adjective and "wished" is a verb. They are not parallel.
(C)	The sentence is not parallel. "Dogmatic" is an adjective and "wished" is a verb and the "he" following the comma creates a run-on.
(D)	Totally parallel. "dogmatism" is a noun and "wish" is a noun and notice the parallel construction of *not from* and *but from*.
(E)	"dogmatism" is a noun and "wished" is a verb. They are not parallel.

Revised Sentence:
The manager's demand that employees follow
health code requirements and wash their hands after
using the restroom <u>resulted not from dogmatism,</u>
<u>but from a wish</u> to keep both employees and
customers healthy.

Correct Answer: (D)

7. Almost 20 years after Elvis Presley won his third

   Grammy <u>for</u> his <u>inspirational</u> performance of the
            A   B
   gospel song *How Great Thou Art,* the nation

   <u>distributing</u> a postage stamp to pay tribute to <u>him</u>.
      C   D
   <u>No error</u>
     E

Did you catch the **Sentence Fragment** with your ear? Let's check the answers one by one.

(A)	"for" is a preposition. Can you *win a Grammy FOR* something? Sure.
(B)	"inspirational" is an adjective modifying the noun "performance."
(C)	While the gerund "distributing" does not need to be changed to the infinitive, it does need to be changed to the simple past tense. The sentence gives us a specific time (20 years after). Changing *distributing* to *distributed* fixes the sentence fragment and **Verb Tense** error.
(D)	"him" refers to Elvis so there is no pronoun ambiguity error. Let's check pronoun case: "him" is an objective pronoun. Does a preposition come before it? Yes! *To him.*

Revised Sentence:

Almost 20 years after Elvis Presley won his third

Grammy <u>for</u> his <u>inspirational</u> performance of the
       A   B

gospel song *How Great Thou Art*, the nation

distributed

<s>distributing</s> a postage stamp to pay tribute to <u>him</u>.
  (C)   D

Verb Tense

<u>No error</u>
  E

Correct Answer: (C)

8. Before women began working in munitions factories

during World War II, the best way for women <u>to earn</u>
                                             A

a living in <u>both</u> England and America <u>has been</u> on the
             B   C

domestic front with labor <u>regarded as</u> "women's work."
                                  D

<u>No error</u>
  E

If you read the sentence in its entirety your ear might catch the **Verb Tense** error, and your eyes should visually catch the "before" at the beginning of the sentence as a tip-off to past perfect. Let's check the answers one by one.

(A)   "to earn" is an infinitive so let's switch it to see if it should be a gerund (earning). Definitely not the fix we need.

(B)   "both" lets us know that we need to look for an "and." We have one: *both England AND America.*

(C)   "has been" is present perfect. But we are not dealing with an action that floated at no set time in the past (they give us the specific time period of WWII), and it isn't an action that continues on into the present (women now have job opportunities that do not involve the domestic front). Notice the "before" and check to see that there are two past actions one happening before the other. Action #1 – *the best way to earn a living has been.* Action #2 – *began working.* Remember that action #1 gets the "had" so *has been* should be changed to *had been.*

(D)   Check the past tense verb "regarded." We are in a specific time in the past (before WWII) so that checks fine. Now check the preposition "as." Can something be *regarded as*? Yes!

Revised Sentence:

Before women began working in munitions factories

during World War II, the best way for women <u>to earn</u>

~~has been~~ *had been* A   *Verb Tense*

a living in <u>both</u> England and America <u>has been</u> on the
        B   (C)

domestic front with labor <u>regarded as</u> "women's work."
                          D

<u>No error</u>
  E

Correct Answer: (C)

9. <u>Among</u> the most dangerous complications that
      A

   women face during pregnancy <u>are</u> "ectopic
                              B

   pregnancy," the dangerous and <u>sometimes deadly</u>
                             C

   occurrence resulting from the improper <u>implantation of</u>
                                     D

   the egg somewhere other than the womb. <u>No error</u>
                                          E

You might not catch the error right off the bat, so let's check each answer choice one by one.

- (A) "among" is a counting word, so we need to make sure it shouldn't be changed to "between." *Among* is used for three or more things and it refers to *most complications*, which is more than two, so among is correct.
- (B) "are" is a present tense verb. We are in the present, so no problem with verb tense, but let's check **SVA**. *Who* or *what* "are" the complications? They only give us one: *ectopic pregnancy*. They never go on to list another, so the plural "are" should be changed to the singular "is." It is a difficult SVA error to catch because in this sentence the subject comes AFTER the verb.
- (C) "sometimes" is an adverb modifying the adjective "deadly." Adverbs do indeed modify adjectives so "sometimes" is correct. "Deadly" modifies the noun "occurrence." Adjectives modify nouns, so "deadly" is also correct.
- (D) "implantation of" sounds awkward and you do want to test that preposition "of." Can you say *implantation of* something? Yes, it's correct. Thank goodness for the obvious **SVA** error in (B); you wouldn't need to spend too much thought on this tricky idiom.

Revised Sentence:

Among the most dangerous complications that
   A   *is*   SVA

women face during pregnancy ~~are~~ "ectopic
                                        Ⓑ

pregnancy," the dangerous and sometimes deadly
                                              C

occurrence resulting from the improper implantation of
                                                       D

the egg somewhere other than the womb. No error
                                                E

Correct Answer: (B)

10. There are a long but concise list of major renovations
          A   B

     to the new house that resulted from the mismanaged
                           C

     efforts of the first contractor. No error
          D   E

Let's check the answers.

- (A) "are" is a simple present tense verb so let's test **SVA**. *What "are"? A long but concise list.* "List" is singular and "are" is plural. That's not a match.
- (B) "but" is a conjunction that flips direction. Are "long" and "concise" opposites? Yes, so the "but" is correct.
- (C) Let's check the preposition "from." Can something *result from* something else? Yes. Make your own sentence: *His insomnia **resulted from** his guilty conscience.*
- (D) Let's check the preposition "of." You can even flip the order of the sentence to test it. *Her grade was a result of her efforts.* Works for me!

Revised Sentence:

       is

There ~~are~~ a long but concise list of major renovations   SVA
    Ⓐ   B

to the new house that resulted from the mismanaged
                      C

efforts of the first contractor. No error
    D   E

Correct Answer: (A)

11. When Anna Webb began to speak out against
              A
     polygamy – she shared her husband, Mormon leader

     Brigham Young, with twenty-six other wives – she
                                           B
     had been the first woman to rebel against the Mormon
        C   D
     practice. No error
                   E

There is a lot going on in this sentence, so let's check the answers one by one.

(A)   The sentence starts with "when" and could possibly be setting up a sentence fragment issue. Get rid of the phrase between the dashes - *she shared her husband, Mormon leader Brigham Young, with twenty-six other wives* - and read the sentence: *When Anna Web began to speak out against polygamy, she had been the first woman to rebel against the Mormon practice.* No sentence fragment issue there. "Began" is a past tense verb. Is the sentence set in the past? Yes. Brigham Young lived in the 1800s and polygamy is now illegal.

(B)   Let's check the preposition "with." Can you *share with* someone? Yes. The adverb "other" is also important. Had the sentence read, *she shared her husband with twenty-six wives,* Anna would be compared to herself. You need the "other" to differentiate.

(C)   "had been" is the past perfect tense. Let's test for a **Verb Tense** error. Are there two past actions? Yes. Is one action happening before the other? No. The "when" indicates that the actions (*began to speak* and *had been*) are occurring simultaneously. *Had been* should be the simple past *became.*

(D)   Should the infinitive "to rebel" be the gerund "rebelling"? Nope.

Revised Sentence:

When Anna Webb began to speak out against
            A
polygamy – she shared her husband, Mormon leader

Brigham Young, with twenty-six other wives – she
  became   B   *Verb Tense*
had been the first woman to rebel against the Mormon
   Ⓒ   D
practice. No error
              E

Correct Answer: (C)

45

12. The area <u>surrounded by</u> the Dodecanese islands to
              A

the south, the Cyclades and Sporades islands to the

west, and a series of Greek and Turkish islands along

the Turkish coast <u>comprise</u> the islands <u>collectively</u>
                       B   C

<u>known as</u> the Northeast Aegean islands. <u>No error</u>
    D   E

Check the answer choices one by one.

   (A)   let's check the preposition "by." Can an area be *surrounded by?* Yes. Make your own
           sentence: *The football star is always **surrounded by** pretty girls.*
   (B)   "comprise" is a simple present tense verb, so let's check **SVA**. *Who* or *what* "comprises"?
           Make sure you cross out the prep phrase *by the Dodecanese islands to the south, the Cyclades
           and Sporades islands to the west, and a series of Greek and Turkish islands along the Turkish
           coast.* Read the sentence without the prep phrase – *The area surrounded comprise....* – "the
           area" is singular and "comprise" is plural so change *comprise* to the singular *comprises.*
   (C)   "collectively" is an adverb modifying the verb "known."
   (D)   check the preposition "as." Can you be *known as* something? Yes. Make your own sentence
           if you are unsure: *She is known as Cha Cha by her friends.*

Revised Sentence:

The area <u>surrounded by</u> the Dodecanese islands to
              A

the south, the Cyclades and Sporades islands to the

west, and a series of Greek and Turkish islands along
                comprises   *SVA*
the Turkish coast ~~comprise~~ the islands <u>collectively</u>
                  (B)   C

<u>known as</u> the Northeast Aegean islands. <u>No error</u>
    D   E

Correct Answer: (B)

13. Because the wind was <u>unusually strong</u>, Caroline
                          A
   finished ten seconds behind her opponent <u>in</u> the relay
                                             B
   race, even though she had <u>ran steadily</u> all the way
                             C
   <u>from</u> the starting line. <u>No error</u>
    D   E

Your ear might be able to catch this one, but be on the safe side and check each of the answer choices.

- (A) "unusually" is an adverb modifying the adjective "strong," which is modifying the noun "wind."
- (B) "in" is a preposition. The expression *in the relay race* works fine. *He won first place in the relay race.*
- (C) "steadily" is an adverb modifying the verb "had ran." That works. "Had ran" is the past perfect, and rightly so, as there are two past actions in the sentence and *running steadily* happens before *finishing ten seconds behind*, BUT even though the tense is right, the past participle "ran" is conjugated incorrectly. Remember, when combined with a linking word you have to use the "u" form of the verb. "Had *ran*" should be "had *run*."
- (D) "from" is a preposition. Can you *run from* something? Yes.

Revised Sentence:

Because the wind was <u>unusually strong</u>, Caroline
                      A
finished ten seconds behind her opponent <u>in</u> the relay
                              run   B   *incorrect past participle*
race, even though she had <u>ran steadily</u> all the way
                          ⓒ

<u>from</u> the starting line. <u>No error</u>
 D   E

Correct Answer: (C)

14. The exercise ball used by physical fitness trainers <u>are</u>
                                                        A
   very effective <u>in activating</u> the electromyographic
                  B
   activity of the abdominal muscles, <u>thereby</u> making
                                       C
   core training <u>during exercise</u> more efficient. <u>No error</u>
                 D   E

ETS is testing one of its favorite errors. **SVA**!

- (A) "are" is a simple present tense verb so let's check SVA. *Who* or *what* "are"? Cross off the prep phrase *by physical fitness trainers*. The sentence now reads: *The exercise ball used are…* So the subject of "are" is "ball." "Ball" is singular and "are" is plural so change the verb to the singular "is."

47

(B)   "in activating" sounds very weird. It is correct, but tempting to declare wrong if you didn't catch the SVA error in (A).

(C)   "thereby" is a conjunction that correctly indicates a cause and effect relationship.

(D)   is "during" the correct preposition? Sure. Make a new sentence. *She sweats during exercise.*

Revised Sentence: *is*

The exercise ball used by physical fitness trainers ~~are~~

                                                                (A)   SVA

very effective <u>in activating</u> the electromyographic
                              B

activity of the abdominal muscles, <u>thereby</u> making
                                                              C

core training <u>during exercise</u> more efficient. <u>No error</u>
                              D   E

Correct Answer: (A)

15. To demand that others do whatever <u>one</u> <u>wants them</u> to
                                                              A   B

     do is often <u>ignoring</u> the wishes and <u>even</u> the needs of
                              C   D

     those who care the most. <u>No error</u>
                                                    E

Let's check the answers.

(A)   "one" is a pronoun. There is no switch to "you" or "we" later in the sentence so it checks out fine.

(B)   "wants" is a simple present tense verb. Check SVA. *Who* "wants"? *One wants.* We have a singular subject (one) and a singular verb (wants) so they check fine. "them" is a plural pronoun that refers to "others" which is also plural.

(C)   "ignoring" is a gerund so check to see if it should be an infinitive instead. Yes! *Ignoring* should be changed to *to ignore,* which is **parallel** to "to demand."

(D)   "even" is used correctly. It is expressing a higher degree.

Revised Sentence:

To demand that others do whatever <u>one</u> <u>wants them</u> to
              to ignore   A   B
do is often <u>ignoring</u> the wishes and <u>even</u> the needs of   *Parallelism*
                    (C)   D
those who care the most. <u>No error</u>
                                        E

Correct Answer: (C)

48

Chapter 4
Pronoun Errors

You've tackled the verbs, which means you've come a long way. The next big chunk of grammar is all about pronouns.

There are three pronoun rules ETS tests: *Pronoun Ambiguity, Pronoun Agreement*, and *Pronoun Case*.

Pronoun Ambiguity is always the easiest to check for, so let's start with it.

Rule #4: Pronoun Ambiguity

How to Find: **Underlined pronouns, especially** *he, she, it, this, that,* **and** *they.*

How to Fix: **Insert the noun that the pronoun should be referencing.**

Let's discuss "it," "this," "that," and "they."

⟶ **Always remember that the noun the pronoun is referring to has to be mentioned somewhere in the sentence.**

For instance: *While walking home from the bakery, Theo tripped and dropped **it** in the mud.*

What is "it"? Perhaps "it" is a cake, or a box of muffins, or even a box of cookies. All of those would be logical, as Theo is walking home from a bakery, but because there is no stated noun in the sentence that the "it" can refer to, the sentence would be considered ambiguous and incorrect.

This option would be better: *While walking home from the bakery carrying a box of cupcakes, Theo tripped and dropped it in the mud.*
- it is now clear that the *it* refers to *a box*.

Try this one: *The company installed two back up power supplies, not wanting power outages to cost it valuable time and money.*
- In this sentence there is only one singular pronoun the "it" could refer to and that is "company." The sentence is correct as written.

⟶ **Sometimes, an "it" or "they" might not be clear because it could refer to more than one singular or plural noun.**

Check it out: *While animal shelters are necessary for abandoned animals, **they** are potentially deadly for older dogs and cats that can't find homes.*

- While it intuitively makes sense that *they* refers to *animal shelters*, grammatically *they* could possibly refer to *animals*, rendering the "they" ambiguous.

> **ETS loves to insert "it" and "they" into a couple of the answer choices of the sentence correction problems. Visually skim through the answer choices. If you see "it" and "they" in one or two of the answer choices, DO NOT pick one of those answers!**

STAY AWAY FROM "IT" AND "THEY"!

⟶ **Another clue that ETS is testing Pronoun Ambiguity is two same gender names followed by a pronoun, such as "he" or "she."**

Let's see how this works:

*Shelly was afraid to tell Linda that Billy had called **her**.*
- Who does the "her" refer to? Is Shelly afraid to say that Billy called *her*, meaning Shelly? Or is Shelly afraid to say that Billy had called *her*, Linda? Maybe Linda and Billy just broke up and Linda doesn't want to hear from him. The "her" is ambiguous.

Rule #5: Pronoun Agreement

How to Find: **Underlined Pronouns.**

How to Fix: **Make the pronoun agree in number with the noun it is referring to.**

We've already discussed pronouns in terms of subject verb agreement (Chapter 3). Remember *each, either, neither*, all the *ones* and *bodys* are singular; *some, all, any, most*, and *none* can be singular or plural; and *who, which*, and *that* can be singular or plural.

Another note to remember is that *collective nouns*, such as the herd, the choir, the government, or any country, such as France, are singular.

Below is a list of additional singular versus plural pronouns.

Singular	*Plural*
he	we
she	they
it	us
this	them
that	these

Let's take a look at some sentences that are testing Pronoun Agreement:

A student must put any books they don't need for class in their locker.

What are the pronouns in the sentence? **_they_** and **_their_**
Are these pronouns singular or plural? plural
What do these pronouns refer to? **_student_**
Do the pronouns match the noun they are referring to? Nope. "Student" is singular so *they* and *their* should be changed to *he or she* and *his or her*. You can actually just pick the gender and stick with it.

Revised sentence: *A student must put any books **he** does not need for class in **his** locker.*

> Notice how the plural "do" is changed to the singular "does." Often, Pronoun Agreement and SVA are tested together.

Take a look at this one: *Everybody must be careful when they cross the street.*

What are the pronouns in the sentence? **_everybody_** and **_they_**
Are these pronouns singular or plural? *everybody* is singular and *they* is plural
What do these pronouns refer to? *they* refers to *everybody*
Do the pronouns match the noun they are referring to? Nope. "Everybody" is singular, so *they* should be changed to *he or she*.

Revised sentence: *Everybody must be careful when **she** crosses the street.*

> We've also changed the plural "cross" to a singular "crosses."

⟶ **Another trick ETS implements when it comes to pronoun agreement is the interchange between *one*, *we*, and *you*.**

ETS might start with "you" and then switch to "one" or "we" later in the sentence. In that case, the pronouns don't agree. You must use the same pronoun throughout!

Take a look at the following examples:

If you want to get good grades, one has to study.

What are the pronouns in the sentence? **_one_** and **_you_**
Do they agree? Nope. Change the *one* to *you* or vice versa.

Revised sentence: *If **you** want to get good grades, **you** have to study.*

Rule #6: Pronoun Case

How to Find: Underlined pronouns.

How to Fix: Change to the correct type of pronoun.

Pronoun Case refers to the type of pronoun used: *Subject Pronouns, Object Pronouns*, or *Possessive Pronouns*.

Subject Pronouns: | I   he   she   we   they   who |

Subject pronouns are the subject of the verb, meaning they are *doing the action*. That's not hard to spot.

Example: *He rode a bike.*

ETS is more likely to test these pronouns in a trickier fashion.

⟶ **Whenever you see a subject pronoun, look BEFORE the pronoun and you must see "than," "like," "as," or forms of the verb "to be" (is, are, was, were, am...).**

Examples: *No one is as mad as he.* ⟶ Look before the "he" and notice the "as."
  Danny is kinder than I. ⟶ Look before the "I" and notice the "than."

Object Pronouns: | me   him   her   us   them   whom |

Object pronouns are the receiving pronouns, aka direct objects.

He gave the ball to me.

"Me" is not doing the action (that is the subject pronoun "he") but is receiving the action (the ball).

⟶ **To test object pronouns look BEFORE the pronoun and you must see a preposition.**

Examples: *...with me...*
  ...to him...
  ...by us...

Take a look at the following:

Are you going to the mall with Sue and I?

First notice the phrase *Sue and.* **Whenever you see a noun (in this case *Sue*) followed by an "and" right before a pronoun (in this case *I*) cross it out.** It is there to distract you!

Now let's read the sentence without the "Sue and."

Are you going to the mall with ~~Sue and~~ I?

That doesn't sound right. It should be - *Are you going to the mall with **me**?*

Let's check it against our rules to make sure.

What word comes directly before the pronoun? <u>**with**</u>
Is "with" a preposition? <u>Yep</u>. So we need the object pronoun "me."

Here's another:

It doesn't matter what country you come from, there is really no fundamental difference between you and me.

What do we get to cross out? <u>***You and***</u>

It doesn't matter what country you come from, there is really no fundamental difference between ~~you and~~ me.

What word comes directly before the pronoun "me?" <u>***between***</u>
Is "between" a preposition? <u>Yep</u>, so the object pronoun "me" is correct.

Possessive Pronouns:

my	his	her	our	their	whose

Possessive pronouns show possession.

*That is **my** pencil.*

No trick there. ETS will test these pronouns in a different manner.

⟶ **Possessive pronouns are directly followed by a gerund (an ing word).**

Take a look:

*Vicky is concerned about **his playing** tennis after spraining his ankle last week.*

This is a confusing one. There is a preposition (about) directly before the first pronoun (his). According to our rules, when a preposition comes before a pronoun it should be an object pronoun. That would change the sentence to - *Vicky is concerned about **him** playing tennis after spraining his ankle last week.* This version of the sentence, however, is wrong. Because a gerund (playing) follows the pronoun "his" it should be kept in the possessive form (his playing). Sounds weird, right? But it is grammatically correct.

Try one on your own. Circle your pick.

*My mom is worried about **me/my** driving without supervision.*

If you picked "my" you are correct! Although the pronoun is preceded by a preposition "about" it is followed by a gerund (driving). The gerund always wins, so it should be the possessive *my*.

*My mom is worried about **my** driving without supervision.*

That's it for pronouns! Let's test our knowledge with a pronoun drill covering Pronoun Ambiguity, Pronoun Agreement, and Pronoun Case.

Pronoun Drill

1. American Girl dolls have entertained and cheered little girls for the last twenty years, and <u>it will be popular to</u> those born in the next decade as well.

   (A) it will be popular to
   (B) they are still popular to
   (C) it is still popular with
   (D) being still popular with
   (E) they will be popular with

2. <u>The roller coaster had a huge drop, this made Bill throw his</u> hands into the air and scream loudly.

   (A) The roller coaster had a huge drop, this made Bill throw his
   (B) Because of how huge the roller coaster's drop was, this is what threw Bill's
   (C) Being a huge drop, Bill found that the roller coaster made him throw his
   (D) The roller coaster, which had a huge drop, throwing Bill's
   (E) The roller coaster's huge drop made Bill throw his

3. Harriet Tubman, an abolitionist <u>which</u> is well
   A
   known for her <u>work with</u> the Underground Railroad,
   B
   first <u>worked</u> for the Union Army as a cook and a
   C
   nurse, and eventually as an armed spy, <u>guiding</u> the
   D
   Combahee River Raid and freeing more than 700

   slaves in South Carolina. <u>No error</u>
   E

4. Some theologians <u>studying</u> the life of Jesus
   A
   <u>have become</u> <u>increasingly</u> interested in the relationship
   B   C
   between his disciples and <u>he</u>. <u>No error</u>
   D   E

5. <u>For most</u> of the twentieth century, people have
   A
   used paper uneconomically, but <u>now that</u> technology
   B
   like the iPad and Kindle are becoming

   <u>increasingly available</u>, environmentalists
   C
   are urging people to change <u>it</u>. <u>No error</u>
   D   E

6. <u>As</u> the author read her poetry to us, she included
   A
   introductions of the poems <u>with stories about</u> her
   B
   <u>own first</u> experiences writing the words,
   C
   <u>offering you</u> a personal glimpse into the author's
   D
   mind. <u>No error</u>
   E

7. <u>In order</u> for the basketball team to believe in and
   A
   <u>be engaged by</u> the new coach, <u>they have</u> to come
   B   C
   across as an experienced <u>expert</u> on the court.
   D
   <u>No error</u>
   E

8. Our new business partners are the <u>most</u>

                                      A

hardworking people we <u>have ever known</u>, and our

                                  B

<u>chief priorities</u>, increasing profit and strengthening

      C

client relations, are similar to <u>them</u>. <u>No error</u>

                            D   E

9. The Toyota Corolla, Honda Accord and Range Rover -

each <u>of these cars</u> <u>was</u> the <u>highest</u> ranked

         A   B   C

in the world at the time <u>they were</u> built. <u>No error</u>

                        D   E

10. The cost of <u>securely disposing</u> of the unused

                  A

medications <u>is roughly</u> <u>two times what</u> the

             B   C

pharmacist paid <u>to purchase it</u>. <u>No error</u>

               D   E

Answers and Explanations

1. American Girl dolls have entertained and cheered
    little girls for the last twenty years, and <u>it will be
    popular to</u> those born in the next decade as well.

    (A) it will be popular to
    (B) they are still popular to
    (C) it is still popular with
    (D) being still popular with
    (E) they will be popular with

There are two errors in this sentence: **Pronoun Agreement** and **Idiom** (I know we haven't discussed Idiom yet, but hang in there). "It" refers to "dolls." "Dolls" is plural so "it" is should be "they." Also, something is not *popular **to** those*, but is *popular **with** those* (the Idiom error).

(B)	"they" is correct but the preposition "to" is incorrect. We are also looking for future tense, not the present tense "are."
(C)	"with" is correct but the pronoun "it" is incorrect, as is the present tense "is."
(D)	"being" is bad. Get rid of it.
(E)	"they" is the correct pronoun and "with" is the correct preposition. We also have the future tense, "will be."

Revised sentence:
American Girl dolls have entertained and cheered
little girls for the last twenty years, and <u>they will be
popular with</u> those born in the next decade as well.

Correct Answer: (E)

2. <u>The roller coaster had a huge drop, this made Bill</u>
   <u>throw his</u> hands into the air and scream loudly.

   (A) The roller coaster had a huge drop, this made
        Bill throw his
   (B) Because of how huge the roller coaster's drop
        was, this is what threw Bill's
   (C) Being a huge drop, Bill found that the roller
        coaster made him throw his
   (D) The roller coaster, which had a huge drop,
        throwing Bill's
   (E) The roller coaster's huge drop made Bill
        throw his

Visually catch the comma followed by the pronoun "this." (…, *this*…) We have a **Run-on**: *The roller coaster had a huge drop* is an independent clause that stands on its own, as is *this made Bill throw his*… There is also an **Ambiguity** error. What is "this"? The "roller coaster" or "the huge drop"?

   (B)   this option is excessively wordy.
   (C)   stay away from "being"!
   (D)   the gerund "throwing" creates a sentence fragment error.
   (E)   fixes the run-on error and removes the ambiguous "this."

Revised sentence:
<u>The roller coaster's huge drop made Bill</u>
<u>throw his</u> hands into the air and scream loudly.

Correct Answer: (E)

3. Harriet Tubman, an abolitionist <u>which</u> is well
                                       A
    known for her <u>work with</u> the Underground Railroad,
                      B
    first <u>worked</u> for the Union Army as a cook and a
              C
    nurse, and eventually as an armed spy, <u>guiding</u> the
                                               D
    Combahee River Raid and freeing more than 700

    slaves in South Carolina. <u>No error</u>
                                   E

Maybe you caught the **Pronoun Agreement** error right away. If not, go through the answer choices one by one.

   (A)   "which" is a pronoun, so we have to first see *who* or *what* it refers to. *An abolitionist.* An
            abolitionist is a person, so we have a pronoun agreement issue. People are modified by "who,"
            not "which."
   (B)   "with" is a preposition. Can you *work with* someone or something? Yes.

(C)   "worked" is a past tense verb. Is the sentence in the past? Yes! While Harriet Tubman *is* still well known (present), she *worked* as a cook and spy in the past.

(D)   "guiding" is a gerund. Should it be "to guide"? Nope, the gerund correctly sets up the dependent clause that follows the comma and is parallel to "freeing."

Revised sentence:

Harriet Tubman, an abolitionist ~~which~~ *who* is well
                                                        (A)

known for her <u>work with</u> the Underground Railroad,
                        B

first <u>worked</u> for the Union Army as a cook and a
                C

nurse, and eventually as an armed spy, <u>guiding</u> the
                                                                   D

Combahee River Raid and freeing more than 700

slaves in South Carolina. <u>No error</u>
                                                    E

Pronoun Agreement

Correct Answer: (A)

4. Some theologians <u>studying</u> the life of Jesus
                                A

    <u>have become</u> <u>increasingly</u> interested in the relationship
             B   C

    between his disciples and <u>he</u>. <u>No error</u>
                                              D   E

Let's check the answer choices one by one to catch the **Pronoun Case** error.

(A)   "studying" is a gerund so let's switch it to an infinitive. *Some theologians **to study** the life of Jesus…*that doesn't work! "Studying" is fine as is.

(B)   "have become" is a present perfect verb. (Notice the use of *have* connected to the past participle *become*.) Is this an action that either floats at no set time in the past or starts in the past but continues on into the present? Yes! *The theologians have become increasingly interested*, which indicates that the interest has been building gradually in the past and continues to grow in the present.

(C)   "increasingly" is an adverb modifying the adjective "interested." That checks fine.

(D)   "he" is a pronoun. Check for pronoun ambiguity. "He" refers to Jesus so no problem there. Jesus is singular and "he" is singular so there is no pronoun agreement error. Let's check for pronoun case. "He" is a subject pronoun. Cross out *his disciples and*; the pronoun phrase is meant to distract you. What word comes before the pronoun "he" now? "Between," which is a preposition. Do subject pronouns follow prepositions? No! Object pronouns do, so change the *he* to *him*. It is common for ETS to try to trick you with a "between" so be on the lookout! It shouldn't be *between Sue and **I**,* it needs to be *between Sue and **me**!*

Revised sentence:

Some theologians <u>studying</u> the life of Jesus
                        A

<u>have become</u> <u>increasingly</u> interested in the relationship
      B   C   *him*   *Pronoun Case*

between his disciples and <u>he</u>. <u>No error</u>
                          (D)   E

Correct Answer: (D)

5. <u>For most</u> of the twentieth century, people have
         A

    used paper uneconomically, but <u>now that</u> technology
                                        B

    like the iPad and Kindle are becoming

    <u>increasingly available</u>, environmentalists
              C

    are urging people to change <u>it</u>. <u>No error</u>
                                 D   E

The "it" should stand out as a red flag. Doesn't mean the "it" is always wrong, but it does mean *it* is under suspicion. We have a **Pronoun Ambiguity** problem.

(A)   is "for most" idiomatically correct? Sure. Check it with your own expression, such as: *for most of my life*... That works.

(B)   is "now that" idiomatically correct? Sure. Again, plug those words into your own expression. *Now that I have graduated*…. That works.

(C)   "increasingly" is an adverb. Is it modifying a verb? Yes. *Are becoming available*. How available? *Increasingly*.

(D)   "it." What the heck is *it?* The iPad, the Kindle, the use of paper? I don't know, so we have an ambiguity error.

Revised sentence:

<u>For most</u> of the twentieth century, people have
    A

used paper uneconomically, but <u>now that</u> technology
                                    B

like the iPad and Kindle are becoming

<u>increasingly available</u>, environmentalists
          C   *their habits*   *Pronoun Ambiguity*

are urging people to change <u>it</u>. <u>No error</u>
                             (D)   E

Correct Answer: (D)

6. <u>As</u> the author read her poetry to us, she included
   A

   introductions of the poems <u>with stories about</u> her
                                    B

   <u>own first</u> experiences writing the words,
           C

   <u>offering you</u> a personal glimpse into the author's
             D

   mind. <u>No error</u>
          E

The **Pronoun Agreement** error might be a hard one to catch without walking through the answer choices one by one.

    (A)   "as" is a preposition. Is *as the author read* legal? Sure. Make your own sentence to check. *As the dog ran…*

    (B)   check the preposition "with." *Included introductions with* works. Check the preposition "about." *Stories about her brother.* Works for me.

    (C)   "own first" sounds a bit awkward, but remember, we can't always go by our ear. It's grammatically correct.

    (D)   Check the "ing" (offering). It works fine; there is no sentence fragment error and it shouldn't be the infinitive "to offer." Now check the "you." Notice that earlier in the sentence the pronoun "us" is used. You can't flip from *us* to *you* so there is a pronoun agreement error.

Revised sentence:
<u>As</u> the author read her poetry to us, she included
 A

introductions of the poems <u>with stories about</u> her
                              B

<u>own first</u> experiences writing the words,
  C   *us*   *Pronoun Agreement*

<u>offering you</u> a personal glimpse into the author's
    (D)

mind. <u>No error</u>
     E

Correct Answer: (D)

7. <u>In order</u> for the basketball team to believe in and
    A

   <u>be engaged by</u> the new coach, <u>they have</u> to come
       B   C

   across as an experienced <u>expert</u> on the court.
                       D

   <u>No error</u>
     E

The **Pronoun Agreement** error might be difficult to catch on the first read-through.

(A)   "in order for" is fine. Make your own sentence. *In order for her to gain weight, Jules learned to cook.*

(B)   cross out the prep phrase *for the basketball team* to simplify the sentence. It now reads: *In order to believe in and be engaged by…* The "to" is distributed to both "believe" and "engaged" and *to believe in* and *be engaged by* are parallel.

(C)   "they" is a pronoun, so let's first check for ambiguity. What could "they" refer to? "Team" is singular, so can't be that, and "coach" is singular so can't be that. The "they" is vague. If it does refer to coach, then we would have a pronoun agreement error. Let's change *they have* to *he has*.

(D)   "expert" is a noun, so let's check for noun agreement. "Coach" is singular and "expert" is singular so they both check.

Revised sentence:

In order for the basketball team to believe in and
  A   *he has*   *Pronoun Agreement / Ambiguity*
be engaged by the new coach, ~~they have~~ to come
   B   (C)
across as an experienced expert on the court.
                            D

No error
  E

Correct Answer: (C)

8. Our new business partners are the <u>most</u>
                                 A

hardworking people we <u>have ever known</u>, and our
                         B

<u>chief priorities</u>, increasing profit and strengthening
      C

client relations, are similar to <u>them</u>. <u>No error</u>
                        D   E

Sometimes your ear will catch the **Pronoun Case** rule. But if you missed it, let's check the answer choices.

(A)   "most" tells us to check for a possible counting error. Should it be "more" instead? I think it is safe to assume that they have met more than two people in their lives, so "most" is correct.

(B)   "have ever known" is a present perfect verb. (Notice the *have* connected to the past participle *known*.) Is this an action that occurred at no set time in the past or that has continued on into the future? Yes! *We have ever known* indicates everyone they've met in the past AND everyone they've met in the present.

(C)   "chief" is an adjective modifying the noun "priorities." Might also want to check for noun agreement. There are two priorities listed: *increasing profit AND strengthening client relations*, so "priorities" should indeed be plural.

(D)   "them" is a pronoun so first check ambiguity. "Them" refers to *business partners* so no ambiguity there. "Partners" is plural and "them" is plural, so there is no pronoun agreement error. Check for pronoun case. This is particularly confusing, as "to" comes before the pronoun. "To" is a preposition, and object pronouns do indeed follow prepositions; however, the sentence should be comparing *our chief priorities* to *THEIR chief priorities*, not to "them," which stands for the *partners*. We can also justify this error as an unclear comparison, which I cover in Chapter 5.

Revised sentence:

Our new business partners are the <u>most</u>
                                   A

hardworking people we <u>have ever known</u>, and our
                           B

<u>chief priorities</u>, increasing profit and strengthening
      C   *theirs*   *Pronoun Case*

client relations, are similar to ~~them~~. <u>No error</u>
                          Ⓓ   E

Correct Answer: (D)

9. The Toyota Corolla, Honda Accord and Range Rover -

each <u>of these cars</u> <u>was</u> the <u>highest</u> ranked
        A   B   C
in the world at the time <u>they were</u> built. <u>No error</u>
                        D   E

Dissect the answer choices to catch the **Pronoun Agreement** error.

    (A)   check the preposition "of" by making your own sentence. *Each of the dogs…* Great, it works. They are indeed "cars," so no problem with the rest of (A).
    (B)   "was" is a simple past tense verb so check SVA. Cross out the prep phrase *of these cars* and realize that the subject of the verb is the singular "each." SVA checks. The tense is fine as well, as we are in a specific time of the past (the time they were built).
    (C)   "highest" is an adverb that describes the action "ranked."
    (D)   "they" is a pronoun, but careful! "They" does not refer to the "cars," rather *they* refers to *each*. We have a pronoun agreement error and *they were* should be changed to *it was*.

Revised sentence:
The Toyota Corolla, Honda Accord and Range Rover -

each <u>of these cars</u> <u>was</u> the <u>highest</u> ranked
        A   B   C *it was*   *Pronoun Agreement/SVA*
in the world at the time ~~they were~~ built. <u>No error</u>
                       Ⓓ   E

Correct Answer: (D)

10. The cost of <u>securely disposing</u> of the unused
$$A$$
     medications <u>is roughly</u> <u>two times what</u> the
$$BC$$
  pharmacist paid <u>to purchase it</u>. <u>No error</u>
$$DE$$

Let's walk through the answer choices step by step to catch the **Pronoun Agreement** error.

     (A)   "securely" is an adverb modifying the verb "disposing."

     (B)   "is" is a singular verb that refers to the subject "the cost." If you didn't catch this and thought that "is" referred to "medications" you forgot to cross out your prep phrase *of the unused medications*. Remember, the subject is NOT going to be inside the preposition. "Roughly" is an adverb modifying the adjective "two."

     (C)   "two times what" is idiomatically correct. Check it by throwing it into our own expression: *This is two times what I thought it would be.*

     (D)   should "to purchase" be "purchasing?" No way! What does the pronoun "it" refer to? *Medications*, which is plural! *It* should be *them.*

Revised sentence:
The cost of <u>securely disposing</u> of the unused
$$A$$
medications <u>is roughly</u> <u>two times what</u> the
$$BC\textit{them}\textit{Pronoun Agreement}$$
pharmacist paid <u>to purchase ~~it~~</u>. <u>No error</u>
$$\boxed{D}E$$

Correct Answer: (D)

Chapter 5
Grammar Rule Mishmash

With verbs and pronouns out of the way, we can move on to the rest of the parts of speech.

Rule #7: Idioms

How to Find: **Underlined Prepositions.**

How to Fix: **Use the correct preposition.**

An idiom is a word or phrase that means something different from its literal interpretation. Take for instance the idiomatic phrase *it's raining cats and dogs;* it isn't REALLY raining cats and dogs, but we are familiar with the gist of the phrase, which indicates it is raining a great amount.

On the SAT however, idioms refer to specific prepositions and and how they connect other words or phrases in the sentence. For example, you are *tolerant **of*** something and have a *responsibility **to*** someone.

Basically, you just have to make sure the correct preposition is used.

This is easier said than done, as sometimes there is no grammatical reason for prepositional idioms to be as they are; it is simply what the grammar gods have ordained. You just have to memorize the correct combination of words.

Think of prepositions as anywhere a rabbit can go in relation to a hill: he can be IN it, ON it, UNDER it, etc.

Let's start with the list of prepositions on the following page.

I've bolded the prepositions that ETS tends to test the most.

aboard	behind	**during**	**of**	**since**	via
about	below	except	**off**	**than**	**with**
above	beneath	excepting	**on**	through	within
across	beside	excluding	onto	**to**	without
after	besides	following	opposite	**toward**	
against	**between**	**for**	outside	**towards**	
along	beyond	**from**	**over**	under	
amid	**but**	**in**	past	underneath	
among	**by**	inside	per	unlike	
around	concerning	into	plus	**until**	
as	considering	**like**	regarding	up	
at	despite	minus	round	upon	
before	down	near	save	versus	

You should also be on the lookout for multi-word prepositions.

according to	due to	in place of	on top of	subsequent to
ahead of	except for	in spite of	out from	that of
as far as	far from	inside of	out of	
as well as	in accordance with	instead of	outside of	
aside from	in addition to	near to	owing to	
because of	in case of	next to	prior to	
by means of	in front of	on account of	pursuant to	
close to	in lieu of	on behalf of	regardless of	

Here's how it works:

Sally has a preoccupation on boys.

What is the preposition? **<u>On</u>**

Ask: *Do you have a preoccupation **on** something?* <u>Nope</u>. *You have a preoccupation **with** something.*

*Sally has a preoccupation **with** boys.*

Here are some common prepositional partners ETS tests:

preoccupation **with**

angered **by** or angry **at**

concerned **about** or concerned **with**

tolerant **of**

worried **about**

prohibited **from**

tolerance **for**

distinguish **from** or distinguish **between** X **and** Y

able **to**

capable **of**

comply **with**

responsible **for**

conscious **of**

equivalent **to**

identical **to**

method **of**

opposed **to**

relevant **to**

attempt **to**

similar **to**

fear **of**

directions **to**

annoyed **by** or annoyed **with**

commentary **on**

authority **on**

with which

parts **to**

indebted **to**

surprised **by**

familiarity **with**

resentful **of**

upset **with**

Following, are some common prepositional pairs.

either...or *(I like **either** yellow **or** blue.)*
neither...nor *(I want **neither** hamburgers **nor** chicken.)*
between...and *(The argument is **between** Richard **and** me.)*

Note: **either, or, neither, between,** *and* **and** *can all be used alone, but* **nor** *cannot be used alone.*

prefer...to *(I **prefer** a day at the spa **to** a night at the movies.)*
no sooner...than *(**No sooner** had I made the reservation **than** he called canceling our date.)*
the reason...is that *(**The reason** Zach cannot have a dog **is that** he is allergic to fur.)*
whether...or *(I was debating **whether** to wear the red dress **or** the blue one.)*
not only...but also *(She **not only** does not want to take chemistry, **but also** does not want to take economics.)*
as...as *(She is **as** fortunate **as** her sister.)*

Let's try it out:

She makes her assistant grade her students' papers so that she is not **prevented to go** *home early.*

Ask*: Are you* prevented *to* go *somewhere? No, you are* prevented *from* going *somewhere.*

Revised sentence: *She makes her assistant grade her students' papers so that she is not* **prevented from going** *home early.*

> **Remember the gerund infinitive switch? All you need is to spot is the infinitive (to go) and check to see if it should be a gerund (from going).**

Rule #8: Unclear Comparisons

How to Find: **Look for the tip-off words** *than, like,* **or** *as.*

How to Fix: **Insert** *that of* **or** *those of* **to make the comparison clear.**

Comparisons are one of the most difficult errors to spot. The following is a simplistic version of an Unclear Comparison error: *His shirt was redder than her.*

Step 1: Spot the "er" word (redder) followed by our tip-off word (than).
Step 2: Ask: *What is this sentence comparing?* It is supposed to be comparing **his shirt** to **her shirt**, but as written the sentence is comparing *his shirt* to *her* (the person), which is not a legit comparison.

Revised sentence: *His shirt was redder than **her shirt.***

Let's try another:

His skin is paler than a ghost.

Step 1: Spot the "er" word (paler) followed by "than."
Step 2: Ask: *What is the sentence comparing?* It is supposed to be comparing *his skin* to *the skin of a ghost*, but as written the sentence compares *his skin* to *a ghost*, and you can't compare apples to oranges, you can only compare oranges to oranges. Insert "that of" to fix.

Revised sentence: *His skin is paler than **that of** a ghost.*

Rule #9: Counting Errors

How to Find: **Look for "er" or "est" words followed by "than."**

How to Fix: **Change the "er" or "est" word to the correct degree.**

Counting Errors Trick #1

⟶ **"Er" words such as faster, greater, and bigger are used to compare exactly two things. "Est" words such as fastest, greatest, and biggest are used to compare three or more things.**

As long as you spot the error, it's the simplest fix in the world! Take a look:

*Of Bob and Tim, Bob is the **smallest**.*

Step 1: Spot the "est" word (smallest).
Step 2: Ask: *How many things are being compared?* <u>Two</u>: **Bob** and ***Tim***
Step 3: Two things takes an "er" word, so change *smallest* to *smaller*.

Revised sentence: *Of Bob and Tim, Bob is the **smaller**.*

Let's try another:

*I have many questions about the meaning of life, but am not sure which is the **more** important.*

Step 1: Spot the "er" word (more).
Step 2: Ask: *How many things are being compared?* <u>Many</u>! ***many questions***
Step 3: More than two things take an "est" word so change *more* to *most*.

Revised sentence: *I have many questions about the meaning of life, but am not sure which is the **most** important.*

Here are some tricky er/est words ETS will use:

er	est
more	most
between	among
better	best
less	least
worse	worst

> **You cannot modify an "er" word with more. For instance, you wouldn't say "more better." Likewise do not modify an "est" word with most - "most best."**

There are adjectives such as "beautiful" that cannot be turned into an "est" word. For example, we can say, *Jane is the more beautiful of the two girls* or *Jane is the most beautiful of the girls in the class.*

Counting Errors Trick #2

Counting nouns are also tested on the SAT. Below is a list of words to use for things that can be counted (such as balls) and things that cannot be counted (such as water).

Can be Counted	Cannot be Counted
fewer	less
number	amount

*Robert puts **less** money in his bank account than Bob does.*

Step 1: Spot the counting word (less).
Step 2: Ask: *What noun is "less" modifying?* **Money**
Step 3: This is a tricky one, because we can count money, but think of it this way: you can count dollar bills, but money as a unit, as with capita, cannot be individually counted. *Less* is correct.

> **Time and distance, like money, are also modified by less.**

*Mark burns **fewer** calories every day since he stopped working out.*

Step 1: Spot the counting word (fewer).
Step 2: Ask: *What noun is "fewer" modifying?* **Calories**
Step 3: Calories can be counted, so *fewer* is correct.

Rule #10: Noun Agreement

How to Find: **Look for underlined nouns.**

How to Fix: **Make sure the noun agrees with however many people or things it refers to.**

Let's look at an example:

*Roger and Veronica bought a new **toothbrush** for their vacation to Hawaii.*

Step 1: Spot the noun (toothbrush). Notice that it is singular.
Step 2: Ask: *Who is buying the toothbrush? Both **Roger and Veronica**.* Are they sharing the same toothbrush? I hope not.
Step 3: Change *a toothbrush* to *toothbrushes*.

Revised sentence: *Roger and Veronica bought new **toothbrushes** for their vacation to Hawaii.*

Let's do one more:

*People who want to be **a doctor** should study hard in school and get good grades.*

Step 1: Spot the noun (doctor).
Step 2: Ask: *To whom does the "doctor" apply?* **People**. Not just one person, but all the people who want to become doctors.
Step 3: Change *a doctor* to *doctors*.

Revised sentence: *People who want to be **doctors** should study hard in school and get good grades.*

Rule #11: Adjective/Adverb

How to Find: **Look for underlined adjectives and underlined adverbs.**

How to Fix: **Change the adjective to an adverb or vice versa.**

We've already covered the difference between adjectives and adverbs in the *Parts of Speech* section of this book. For a refresher, remember **adjectives modify nouns, and adverbs modify verbs, adjectives, and other adverbs.**

> **Many adverbs end in "ly."**

But remember, there are some adverbs that **do not** end in "ly" (earlier, faster, late, less...) and there are some *adjectives* that do (lovely, lonely, motherly, friendly...).

Let's see how ETS tests this grammar rule:

*Lou has been called fickle due to his **constant** changing preferences.*

Step 1: Spot the adjective "constant."
Step 2: Ask: *What is the adjective modifying?* <u>**Changing**</u>.
Step 3: Ask: *What part of speech is changing?* <u>It's an adjective!</u> "Changing" is modifying "preferences," which is a noun.
Step 4: Change *constant* to the adverb *constantly* because adverbs modify adjectives.

Revised sentence: *Lou has been called fickle due to his **constantly** changing preferences.*

How about this one:

*Jessica describes her trip to Africa **vividly** in her memoir.*

Step 1: Spot the adverb (vividly).
Step 2: Ask: *What is vividly modifying?* <u>**Describes**</u>. HOW she describes. *Describes* is a verb and adverbs modify verbs so the sentence is correct as is.

Rule #12: Double Negatives

How to Find: **Look for the tip-off words *hardly, barely, scarcely, none*, or *but* in conjunction with a *not* or *no*.**

How to Fix: **Either change the *not* or *no* to *any*, or remove the *hardly, barely, scarcely, none*, or *but*.**

Double negatives are easy to catch with the ear because they sound so wrong. Read the following out loud:

Lucy has hardly no friends.

Step 1: Spot the "hardly no."
Step 2: We have a double negative on our hands so change the *no* to *any*, or remove the *hardly*.

Revision 1: *Lucy has **hardly any** friends.*
Revision 2: *Lucy has **no** friends.*

He can't go to Hawaii without hardly any money.

Step 1: Spot the "without hardly any."
Step 2: We have a double negative error so change the *without* to *with*, or remove the *hardly*.

Revision 1: *He can't go to Hawaii **with hardly any** money.*
Revision 2: *He can't go to Hawaii **without any** money.*

Rule #13: Conjunctions

How to Find: **Look for underlined conjunctions.**

How to Fix: **Change to the correct conjunction.**

We have already reviewed conjunctions in the *Parts of Speech* section of this book. For a refresher, the most common conjunctions are: **or, by, and, but, yet, so, because**.

Remember, conjunctions are either carrying the sentence along in the same direction (and, so....) or they are flipping the direction of the sentence (but, although...) OR indicating cause and effect (because, since...)

Let's try some:

*She wanted to go to a good college, **and** she got horrible grades in high school.*

Step 1: Spot the conjunction (and).
Step 2: Ask: *Is the sentence flowing in the same direction or a different direction?* The sentence is actually flipped. *Wanting to go to* college and *getting horrible grades* are not along the same lines. We need a flip word, such as "but."

Revised sentence: *She wanted to go to a good college, **but** she got horrible grades in high school.*

*Tara studied for her physics test in the library; **however**, it was difficult to concentrate because of the couple whispering incessantly at the table across from her.*

Step 1: Spot the conjunction (however).
Step 2: Ask: *Is the sentence flipping direction?* Yes, it is. She is studying, BUT getting distracted. The "however" is correct.

The construction of the however following a semicolon seems funky, but is totally correct, so memorize the visual – "blah, blah, blah; *however,* blah, blah, blah."

Your teacher may have taught you that it is not okay to start a sentence with "because." It is absolutely okay to start a sentence with "because." In fact, a sentence that begins with "because" is often the right answer, as ETS knows students are warned against the "because." Why do teachers discourage against the use of "because" at the start of a sentence? The word "because" often forms an incomplete sentence when it is used to answer a question. For example, "Why did Barack Obama run for president? Because he thought he could change the world." In that example, the word "because" turns a perfectly good complete sentence ("He thought he could change the world") into an incomplete sentence. Thus, it is NOT okay to begin sentences with "because" if it creates an incomplete sentence.

Because her dad works so much, she rarely gets to see him.

The sentence above is grammatically correct and ETS approved.

Rule #14: Misplaced Modifier

How to Find: **An intro phrase, especially an "ing" phrase, followed by a comma.**

How to Fix: **Move the correct noun directly after the modifying phrase (or after the comma).**

Take a look at a classic ETS misplaced modifier error:

Running through the park, a walnut fell from a tree and hit Michael on the head.

Step 1: Spot the intro "ing" phrase followed by a comma. (Running through the park).
Step 2: Ask: *What noun directly follows the intro phrase?* <u>**Walnut**</u>. Whatever noun follows the modifying phrase is the noun that is being modified. This would mean that the *walnut was running through the park*. That's NOT ETS's intended meaning.
Step 3: Ask: *What noun is ETS really trying to modify?* <u>**Michael**</u>. Michael is the person who is running through the park.
Step 4: Move the correct noun (Michael) directly after the modifying phrase.

Revised sentence: ***Running through the park, Michael*** *was hit on the head by a walnut that fell from a tree.*

Here's another:

Terrified of the water, Cynthia's fear prevented her from swimming in the ocean.

Step 1: Spot the intro phrase followed by a comma (Terrified of the water).
Step 2: Ask: *Who or what is terrified of the water?* Whatever comes after the introductory phrase! <u>**Cynthia's fear.**</u> Can Cynthia's fear be terrified of the water? Nope, but **Cynthia** can.
Step 3: Move the correct noun (Cynthia) after the modifying phrase.

Revised sentence: ***Terrified of the water, Cynthia*** *was prevented from swimming in the ocean due to her fear.*

> **Sometimes the best way to fix a misplaced modifier error is to change the verb in the modifying phrase.**

Let's see how this works:

Based on a comprehensive study, scientists now declare vitamin C a necessary component of collagen formation.

Step 1: Spot the intro phrase followed by a comma (Based on a comprehensive study).
Step 2: Ask: *Who or what is based on the comprehensive study?* According to the sentence as written, **<u>*scientists*</u>**. But *scientists* CANNOT be *based on a study*.
Step 3: Let's change the verb in the modifying phrase to *relying*.

Revised sentence: **Relying** *on a comprehensive study,* **scientists** *now declare vitamin C a necessary component of collagen formation.*

Rule #15: Run-On Sentences

How to Find: **Look for a comma splice.**
* ***The coach likes to yell at his players, he thinks such a tactic incites them to work harder.***

How to Fix: **Insert a conjunction after the comma or replace the comma with a semicolon.**

Or look for two independent clauses that are not properly connected.
* ***Bill likes to dance he is a professional salsa dancer.***

How to Fix: **Insert a semicolon or insert a comma followed by a conjunction.**

Let's take a look at the comma splice.

⟶ **The visual clue is an independent clause, followed by a comma, followed by a pronoun, such as *he, she, they, it,* or *this*.**

Working out at least three times a week is the key to a healthy heart, it also ensures a fit, more lean body.

Step 1: Spot the visual: ("*...heart, it…*") We have two independent clauses. *Working out at least three times a week is the key to a healthy heart* (a sentence that can stand perfectly well on its own two feet) and *it also ensures a fit, more lean body* (another sentence that exists independently).
Step 2: Insert a conjunction, or remove the comma and insert a semicolon.

Revision 1: *Working out at least three times a week is the key to a healthy heart,* **and** *it also ensures a fit, more lean body.*
Revision 2: *Working out at least three times a week is the key to a healthy heart; it also ensures a fit, more lean body.*

A dependent clause or a phrase followed by a comma is perfectly okay.

Take a look:

* ***With no chance of parole, the convict accepted his fate glumly.***

The phrase, *with no chance of parole*, cannot stand on its own as a complete sentence, so should be followed by a comma and the subsequent independent clause (the convict accepted his fate glumly).

Here is another example of a run-on sentence:

Carol loved playing tennis she thought today was too hot.

Step 1: Notice that the sentence is actually made up of two independent clauses that are not properly connected: *Carol loved playing tennis* and *she thought today was too hot.*

Step 2: Fix the run-on by adding a comma and a conjunction, or inserting a semicolon with a "however."

Revision 1: *Carol loved playing tennis**, but** she thought today was too hot.*
Revision 2: *Carol loved playing tennis**; however,** she thought today was too hot.*

Rule #16: Sentence Fragments

How to Find: **Look for the tip-off words *if*, *since*, or *whether* starting the sentence.**

How to Fix: **Remove the *if, since*, or *whether*.**

Sentence Fragments are all over the Sentence Correction portion of the SAT grammar section, and occasionally on the Error IDs and Improving Paragraphs. You have to read the sentences carefully, because the best way to catch a sentence fragment error is to HEAR IT.

Let's try one: ***Since** some hotels charge hidden fees, such as a fifteen dollar resort fee tacked onto the bill, but others are upfront with all the costs.*

Step 1: Spot the tip-off word (since).

Step 2: Let your ear catch the fact that the sentence never wraps itself up. *Since they charge hidden fees, but others don't....* so what? There would be no problem if the sentence read: *Since some hotels charge hidden fees, such as a fifteen dollar resort fee tacked onto the room bill, but others are upfront with all the costs, my family always asks about hidden fees before making any hotel reservations.*

Step 3: The simplest fix (and the only fix on an Error ID question) is to remove the "since."

Revised sentence: *Some hotels charge hidden fees, such as a fifteen dollar resort fee tacked onto the bill, but others are upfront with all the costs.*

Here's another sentence fragment trick:

Reminiscent of the black and white film noir flicks, "Hollywoodland" starring Diane Lane, Adrien Brody, and Ben Affleck.

Step 1: Spot the sentence fragment error. What about "Hollywoodland"? The sentence never wraps itself up.
Step 2: Change the "ing" *starring* to *stars*.

Revised sentence: *Reminiscent of the black and white film noir flicks, "Hollywoodland" **stars** Diane Lane, Adrien Brody, and Ben Affleck.*

Watch out for those awkward "ings." They often create sentence fragment errors!

Rule #17: Passive versus Active

Constructing a sentence in passive voice is NOT grammatically wrong, but ETS DOES frown upon it. ALWAYS CHOSE ACTIVE IF YOU HAVE THE CHOICE!

Passive: *The meal was cooked by her.*
Active: *She cooked the meal.* (Ah…much better, because the subject, "she" is doing the action "cooked.")

> **Also be on the lookout for the use of nouns, when the use of verbs would make the sentence less wordy.**

Don't construct a sentence that reads, *"Her diabetes prevents her from **the consumption of** too much sugar."*

Get rid of the noun (consumption) and change it to an active verb (consuming).

Revised sentence: *Her diabetes prevents her **from consuming** too much sugar.*

Rule #18: Redundancy

Redundancy has not been tested as frequently on recent SAT tests as it has in the past.

Redundancy means A LITERAL REPETITION OF WORDS.

Redundancy is not the same thing as wordiness.

What makes redundancy so tricky to spot is that ETS will separate the repetitive words or phrases with a whole bunch of junk in between.

For example: *The annual election for student body president is held every year in March.*

Did you catch the redundancy error? *Annual* and *every year* are repetitive. To fix either remove "annual" or "every year."

Revised Sentence: *The **annual** election for student body president is held in March.*

Here's a common redundancy: *On the previous test before this one, Kristen scored an A.*

Previous and *before this one* are redundant. Eliminate one or the other.

Revised Sentence: *On the **previous** test, Kristen scored an A.*

Let's try one more:

The attorney tried to give his partner a rough approximation of how many jurors were screened for the panel.

ETS doesn't separate the redundant phrase in the above sentence: *rough approximation*.

Revised Sentence: *The attorney tried to give his partner* **an approximation** *of how many jurors were screened for the panel.*

⟶ **There are certain words that are considered *absolute words*, and cannot be modified by the adverbs "more" or "very."**

⟶ **Absolute Words: *straight, perfect, round, unique***

You cannot say *more straight*, but you can say *more **nearly** straight*.

Rule #19: Diction

How to Find: **Difficult vocab words, or words that are similar in spelling to other words.**

How to Fix: **Change to the correct word.**

Who hasn't been confused by *effect* versus *affect*? (The majority of the time *effect* is a noun, as in *the result*, and *affect* is a verb, as in *to influence. While this might not ALWAYS be the case, it is the way these two words will be tested on the SAT.*).

Diction errors have been increasingly less prevalent throughout the years, but you should still be on the lookout in case ETS decides to be extra sneaky.

Here are some common Diction Errors:

Dual (two) vs. **Duel** (to fight)
Principle (an idea or rule of conduct) vs. **Principal** (most important (adj.), a person in charge (noun), or sum of money (noun))

Compliment (a flattering comment) vs. **Complement** (to go together well)
Allusion (a reference) vs. **Illusion** (a false impression)
Stationary (not moving) vs. **Stationery** (the paper)
Except (excluding) vs. **Accept** (to say yes to something)
Respectfully (with respect) vs. **Respectively** (correspondingly)
Rise (to go up) vs. **Raise** (to lift up)
Incredible (hard to believe, extraordinary) vs. **Incredulous** (disbelieving)
Desert (a dry place) vs. **Dessert** (the sweet)
Site (a place) vs. **Cite** (to reference)

That's it for the grammar rules!

Let's see how you did with the mishmash by scattering the rules throughout the next drill.

Sentence Correction
Mishmash Drill

1. The British Medical Journal recently publishing a study about a new blood test for pregnant women that can accurately assess genetic disorders and complications in an unborn child.

   (A) The British Medical Journal recently publishing a study
   (B) A study recently published by the British Medical Journal
   (C) The British Medical Journal recently would publish a study
   (D) The British Medical Journal recently published a study
   (E) Recently publishing a study, the British Medical Journal

2. The most common types of injuries in football are sprains, strains, and bruises, since such is the case, most football players warm up and condition before a game.

   (A) bruises, since such is the case, most football players warm up and condition before a game
   (B) bruises; therefore, most football players warm up and condition before a game
   (C) bruises, with most football players therefore warming up and conditioning before a game
   (D) bruises, most football players warm up and condition before a game as a result.
   (E) bruises; and most football players warm up and condition before a game

3. In spite of his handicap, the theoretical physicist Professor Stephen Hawking worked on his theorems of relativity and numerous publications almost every day, and he was becoming a noted academic celebrity and well-respected scientist.

   (A) and he was becoming
   (B) becoming
   (C) where he became
   (D) when he became
   (E) to become

4. Jane Fonda rose to fame as an actress, model, and fitness guru, being Henry Fonda's daughter.

   (A) Jane Fonda rose to fame as an actress, model, and fitness guru, being Henry Fonda's daughter
   (B) Being Jane Fonda, Henry Fonda's daughter rose to fame as an actress, model, and fitness guru
   (C) Jane Fonda rose to fame as an actress, model, and fitness guru, and she was Henry Fonda's daughter
   (D) Jane Fonda, who as Henry Fonda's daughter rose to fame as an actress, model, and fitness guru
   (E) Jane Fonda, Henry Fonda's daughter, rose to fame as an actress, model, and fitness guru

5. Aware of the growing popularity of Google as a source of medical information, <u>doctors warn that using advice found on the Internet to treat ailments may</u> lead to further complications.

   (A) doctors warn that using advice found on the Internet to treat ailments may
   (B) doctors warning that using advice found on the Internet to treat ailments would
   (C) and with warnings from doctors that using advice found on the Internet to treat ailments may
   (D) using advice found on the Internet to treat ailments, this is what experts warn may
   (E) warnings from doctors concerning using advice found on the Internet to treat ailments may

6. Watts and Compton <u>are an example of neighborhoods that</u> have a shortage of adequately staffed schools.

   (A) are an example of neighborhoods that
   (B) are examples of neighborhoods that
   (C) are examples where neighborhoods
   (D) exemplify a neighborhood that
   (E) exemplify neighborhoods where they

7. Given the price of admission to a movie, <u>the cost of it typically floats</u> around $13, many people say, "I'll wait for the movie to come out on DVD."

   (A) the cost of it typically floats
   (B) and typically it floats at a cost
   (C) which typically floats
   (D) in that it typically floats
   (E) they typically float

8. <u>There is</u> progressively more dependency on text messages, some people still refuse to text, especially those who prefer to talk to someone on the phone.

   (A) There is
   (B) There are
   (C) Because there are
   (D) In that there is
   (E) Although there is

9. The complex verse and intermingling of past, present, and future in Faulkner's writing strike many readers as both frustrating <u>but</u> decidedly genius.

   (A) but
   (B) and
   (C) but also
   (D) and as
   (E) yet

10. Nutritionists have found that complex carbohydrates <u>are most likely to provide essential nutrients than simple carbohydrates.</u>

   (A) are most likely to provide essential nutrients than simple carbohydrates
   (B) are more likely to provide essential nutrients compared to simple carbohydrates
   (C) are more likely than simple carbohydrates to provide essential nutrients
   (D) compared with simple carbohydrates most likely provide essential nutrients
   (E) more likely provide essential nutrients than in simple carbohydrates

11. <u>The ancient Greeks had a frugal diet and ate mostly wheat, olive oil, and wine, they</u> managed to make the most of agricultural hardship by creating varied meals with these three staples.

   (A) The ancient Greeks had a frugal diet and ate mostly wheat, olive oil, and wine, they
   (B) Because the ancient Greeks had a frugal diet made up of mostly wheat, olive oil, and wine, they
   (C) What with a frugal diet being made up of mostly wheat, olive oil, and wine, the ancient Greeks
   (D) The ancient Greeks, who had a frugal diet and ate mostly wheat, olive oil, and wine, and
   (E) With a frugal diet and them eating mostly wheat, olive oil, and wine, the ancient Greeks

12. The Scripps National Spelling Bee attracts students <u>having mastered</u> words that the majority of adults do not yet know how to spell, such as menhir and apodyterium.

(A) having mastered
(B) for mastering
(C) who have mastered
(D) to be mastering
(E) and they mastered

13. Although he wrote over 2500 years ago, the Greek playwright Sophocles is still being <u>read, his plays are</u> performed on stages all over the world.

(A) read, his plays are
(B) read; his plays being
(C) read: his plays are being
(D) read; his plays are
(E) read, yet his plays are

14. When walking down the aisle, <u>not stepping on her train and tripping should be the bride's primary concern.</u>

(A) not stepping on her train and tripping should be the bride's primary concern
(B) not stepping on her train and tripping should be what primarily concerns the bride
(C) the train and not tripping on it should be the bride's primary concern
(D) the bride should be primarily concerned with not stepping on her train and tripping
(E) the bride, regarding not stepping on her train and tripping, should be primarily concerned

15. A severe case of pneumonia suddenly hit Rachel on her birthday, February 12th, preventing her from attending her own birthday party in the <u>evening, the guests were not warned because of Rachel being so sick.</u>

(A) evening, the guests were not warned because of Rachel being so sick
(B) evening; not warning the guests because Rachel was so sick
(C) evening, because Rachel was so sick, the guests were not warned
(D) evening; the guests were not warned because Rachel was so sick
(E) evening and not warning the guests, which was caused by Rachel being so sick

Answers and Explanations

1. <u>The British Medical Journal recently publishing a study</u> about a new blood test for pregnant women that can accurately assess genetic disorders and complications in an unborn child.

    (A) The British Medical Journal recently publishing a study
    (B) A study recently published by the British Medical Journal
    (C) The British Medical Journal recently would publish a study
    (D) The British Medical Journal recently published a study
    (E) Recently publishing a study, the British Medical Journal

Did you identify the error when you read through the sentence? It is a **Sentence Fragment** error created by the awkward "ing" (publishing).

(B)	gets rid of the awkward "ing" by changing "publishing" to "published," but the sentence is still a fragment. It leaves us asking: *What about the study that was published?*
(C)	"would publish" is the wrong tense. It should just be "published."
(D)	gives us the "published" we've been looking for. When we read the sentence we can hear the difference. The sentence is now complete.
(E)	rearranges the sentence incorrectly. "*...the British Medical Journal about a new blood test...*" makes no sense.

Revised sentence:

<u>The British Medical Journal recently published a study</u> about a new blood test for pregnant women that can accurately assess genetic disorders and complications in an unborn child.

Correct Answer: (D)

2. The most common types of injuries in football are sprains, strains, and <u>bruises, since such is the case, most football players warm up and condition before a game.</u>

(A) bruises, since such is the case, most football players warm up and condition before a game
(B) bruises; therefore, most football players warm up and condition before a game
(C) bruises, with most football players therefore warming up and conditioning before a game
(D) bruises, most football players warm up and condition before a game as a result.
(E) bruises; and most football players warm up and condition before a game

The sentence as written is a **Run-on**. *The most common types of injuries in football are sprains, strains, and bruises* – is an independent sentence that stands on its own and *since such is the case, most football players warm up and condition before a game*, is also a complete sentence that stands on its own.

(B)   fixes the run-on by inserting a semi-colon. The sentence is also less wordy with the use of "therefore" instead of "since such is the case."

(C)   by inserting a "with" after the comma we have fixed the run-on error, but created a misplaced modifier error.

(D)   we still have a run-on. Spot the visual clue ("...bruises, most...")

(E)   had there been a comma and then a conjunction, such as "so" we would be in business, but the "and" is the wrong conjunction because it doesn't indicate the cause and effect relationship. Also, the semicolon takes the place of a conjunction so you wouldn't use both. Look out for that visual tip-off ("...; and...") to spot the error.

Revised sentence:

The most common types of injuries in football are sprains, strains, and <u>bruises; therefore, most football players warm up and condition before a game.</u>

Correct Answer: (B)

3. In spite of his handicap, the theoretical physicist
   Professor Stephen Hawking worked on his theorems
   of relativity and numerous publications almost
   every day, <u>and he was becoming</u> a noted academic
   celebrity and well-respected scientist.

   (A) and he was becoming
   (B) becoming
   (C) where he became
   (D) when he became
   (E) to become

We have a **Wordy Awkward "ing"** in this sentence. Past progressive is not the correct tense and we do not need the "and" after the comma, as the first half of the sentence should be followed by a dependent clause.

(B)	"becoming" ushers in a dependent clause that connects to the first half of the sentence beautifully and fixes the wordiness issue.
(C)	the "where" refers to "every day" and "every day" is not a place, so the pronoun "where" is incorrect.
(D)	"when" refers to "every day" and although it correctly refers to a period of time, Hawkings did not work on his theorems every day WHEN he became a celebrity, he worked on them EVEN BEFORE he became a celebrity, so the intended meaning of the sentence is changed.
(E)	you wouldn't want to stick an infinitive after a comma, and the comma is not underlined, which means the comma is there to stay. "To become" also changes the meaning of the sentence, indicating that he worked every day in order to become a noted celebrity, as opposed to his notoriety being a bi-product of his work.

Revised sentence:

In spite of his handicap, the theoretical physicist
professor Stephen Hawking worked on his theorems
of relativity and numerous publications
almost every day, <u>becoming</u> a noted academic
celebrity and well respected scientist.

Correct Answer: (B)

4. <u>Jane Fonda rose to fame as an actress, model,</u>
   <u>and fitness guru, being Henry Fonda's daughter.</u>

   (A) Jane Fonda rose to fame as an actress,
       model, and fitness guru, being Henry
       Fonda's daughter
   (B) Being Jane Fonda, Henry Fonda's daughter
       rose to fame as an actress, model, and fitness
       guru
   (C) Jane Fonda rose to fame as an actress, model,
       and fitness guru, and she was Henry Fonda's
       daughter
   (D) Jane Fonda, who as Henry Fonda's daughter
       rose to fame as an actress, model, and fitness
       guru
   (E) Jane Fonda, Henry Fonda's daughter, rose to
       fame as an actress, model, and fitness guru

We have a **Wordy Awkward** sentence here due to the "being." Remember: ***being is bad!***

   (B)   it has a "being." Get rid of it!
   (C)   this answer choice slightly changes the intended meaning. The sentence indicates that there is
            a certain cause and effect relationship. Jane Fonda *rose to fame* in part because *she is Henry*
            Fonda's daughter, and using a comma with the conjunction "and" removes this cause and effect
            relationship.
   (D)   creates a sentence fragment. Can you hear it? *What about Jane Fonda?* The sentence never
            gets around to telling us.
   (E)   clear and concise, (E) is the best answer. Remember, you can clear away the phrase between
            the two commas (*Henry Fonda's daughter*) to test the sentence: *Jane Fonda rose to fame as*
            an actress, model, and fitness guru.

Revised sentence:

<u>Jane Fonda, Henry Fonda's daughter,</u>
<u>rose to fame as an actress, model, and</u>
<u>fitness guru.</u>

Correct Answer: (E)

5. Aware of the growing popularity of Google as a source of medical information, <u>doctors warn that using advice found on the Internet to treat ailments may</u> lead to further complications.

(A) doctors warn that using advice found on the Internet to treat ailments may
(B) doctors warning that using advice found on the Internet to treat ailments would
(C) and with warnings from doctors that using advice found on the Internet to treat ailments may
(D) using advice found on the Internet to treat ailments, this is what experts warn may
(E) warnings from doctors concerning using advice found on the Internet to treat ailments may

Notice that intro phrase followed by a comma (*Aware of the growing popularity of Google as a source of medical information*). We may have a **Misplaced Modifier** error. Let's check it. Ask: *Who or what is aware of the growing popularity of Google as a source of medical information?* Your answer is right after the comma (doctors). Well that makes sense. *Doctors are aware of this phenomenon and are warning against it.* Check the other answer choices to make sure there isn't another error you may have missed.

(B)   ETS inserts the awkward "ing" (warning) and changes "may" to "would" which creates a verb tense error.

(C)   "and with warnings…" creates a sentence fragment error.

(D)   creates a modifying error and a run-on! What's aware? *Using advice.* Notice the visual tip-off: (*"…ailments, this…"*) This option is way wordy and wrong!

(E)   creates a modifying error. Now *warnings from doctors* are aware of the Google phenomenon, and "warnings" cannot be aware.

Correct Answer: (A)

6. Watts and Compton <u>are an example of neighborhoods that</u> have a shortage of adequately staffed schools.

(A) are an example of neighborhoods that
(B) are examples of neighborhoods that
(C) are examples where neighborhoods
(D) exemplify a neighborhood that
(E) exemplify neighborhoods where they

Once you've seen a couple at work, **Noun Agreement** errors become much easier to spot. *Watts and Compton* is a compound subject so the plural "are" works. Notice the noun "example." What is an *example*? *Watts* AND *Compton. Example* should be *examples* because we have two neighborhoods.

(B)   we have the plural noun "examples," so this answer choice correctly fixes the noun agreement error.

(C)   the noun agreement error is fixed, but removing the "of" and inserting the "where" changes the meaning of the sentence.

(D)   "exemplify" is a plural verb and "Watts and Compton" is a plural compound subject so SVA works. "A neighborhood" refers to ONE neighborhood, not TWO, so we still have a noun agreement error.

(E)   "exemplify" is a plural verb matching the plural compound subject "Watts and Compton," but who the heck is "they"? Beware of ambiguous pronouns!

Revised sentence:

Watts and Compton <u>are examples of neighborhoods that</u> have a shortage of adequately staffed schools.

Correct Answer: (B)

7. Given the price of admission to a movie, <u>the cost of it typically floats</u> around $13, many people say, "I'll wait for the movie to come out on DVD."

(A) the cost of it typically floats
(B) and typically it floats at a cost
(C) which typically floats
(D) in that it typically floats
(E) they typically float

There are several errors with this sentence as written, but let's focus on the **Redundancy** error. In the non-underlined portion of the sentence we see "price" and in the underlined portion we see "cost." *Price* and *cost* mean the same thing and are redundant.

(B)   we have that ambiguous, unnecessary "it" and we still have "cost," which is redundant to "price."

(C)   "which" refers to price and is both idiomatically correct and fixes the redundancy error. "Floats" is a singular verb that refers to the singular subject "price" so SVA checks fine as well. Notice also how this is the least wordy answer choice.

(D)   what is "it"? The movie, the price? We just can't be sure. While *in that it* is a grammatically correct phrase, it is not idiomatically correct as used in this sentence.

(E)   who the heck is "they"? Also, "price" is singular.

Revised sentence:

Given the price of admission to a movie, <u>which typically floats</u> around $13, many people say, "I'll wait for the movie to come out on DVD."

Correct Answer (C)

8. <u>There is</u> progressively more dependency on text messages, some people still refuse to text, especially those who prefer to talk to someone on the phone.

(A) There is
(B) There are
(C) Because there are
(D) In that there is
(E) Although there is

At first glance, ETS seems to be testing SVA, but the sentence actually contains a **Run-on** error. Check the simple present tense verb "is." *Who* or *what* "is"? *Dependency*. Singular verb and singular subject checks. But look at the non-underlined portion of the sentence. *There is progressively more dependency on text messages* is a complete phrase that can stand on its own and *some people still refuse to text* is also a complete sentence that can stand on its own. We have a run-on.

(B) "are" is plural and "dependency" is singular.
(C) "because there are" doesn't form the right relationship. *People are not refusing to text* BECAUSE *there is more dependency*. Also, the "are" should be "is."
(D) "In that there is" doesn't form the right relationship between the *growing dependency* and the *refusal to text*.
(E) "although there is" sets up the right relationship. *There is a dependency on texts* BUT *some people still refuse to text*. We need a conjunction that sets up the flip in the sentence.

Revised sentence:

<u>Although there is</u> progressively more dependency on text messages, some people still refuse to text, especially those who prefer to talk to someone on the phone.

Correct Answer: (E)

9. The complex verse and intermingling of past, present, and future in Faulkner's writing strike many readers as both frustrating <u>but</u> decidedly genius.

(A) but
(B) and
(C) but also
(D) and as
(E) yet

ETS is testing **Idiom**. Spot the "both" and the underlined "but" and remember that *both* always goes with *and*.

(B) we have a winner. "Both" should be paired with "and."
(C) "both" does not go with "but also."

(D)   "both" does not go with "and as."

(E)   "both" does not go with "yet."

Revised sentence:

The complex verse and intermingling of past, present, and future in Faulkner's writing strike many readers as both frustrating <u>and</u> decidedly genius.

Correct Answer: (B)

10. Nutritionists have found that complex carbohydrates <u>are most likely to provide essential nutrients than simple carbohydrates.</u>

   (A) are most likely to provide essential nutrients than simple carbohydrates

   (B) are more likely to provide essential nutrients compared to simple carbohydrates

   (C) are more likely than simple carbohydrates to provide essential nutrients

   (D) compared with simple carbohydrates most likely provide essential nutrients

   (E) more likely provide essential nutrients than in simple carbohydrates

There are a couple errors in the sentence as written. There is a **Counting Error** and the **Comparison** is **Unclear**. Check the word "most." *Most* compares three or more things. How many things are being compared? Two: *complex carbohydrates* and *simple carbohydrates*. "Most" should be "more."

   (B)   the construction of the comparison is off. We have a "more," which is correct, but the *more* needs to be combined with a *than* rather than a "compared to."

   (C)   we have a "more" and it is connected to a "than," so even though the sentence might sound a bit awkward it is grammatically correct.

   (D)   we have a "most" instead of a "more" so we can eliminate (D).

   (E)   "than in" is not idiomatically correct as used in this sentence.

Revised sentence:

Nutritionists have found that complex carbohydrates <u>are more likely than complex simple carbohydrates to provide essential nutrients.</u>

Correct Answer: (C)

11. <u>The ancient Greeks had a frugal diet and ate</u>
    <u>mostly wheat, olive oil, and wine, they</u> managed
    to make the most of agricultural hardship by
    creating varied meals with these three staples.

    (A) The ancient Greeks had a frugal diet and ate
        mostly wheat, olive oil, and wine, they
    (B) Because the ancient Greeks had a frugal diet
        made up of mostly wheat, olive oil, and
        wine, they
    (C) What with a frugal diet being made up of
        mostly wheat, olive oil, and wine, the
        ancient Greeks
    (D) The ancient Greeks, who had a frugal diet
        and ate mostly wheat, olive oil, and wine,
        and
    (E) With a frugal diet and them eating mostly
        wheat, olive oil, and wine, the ancient
        Greeks

Notice the visual clue of the comma followed by "they" (*"..., they..."*). ETS has given us another **Run-on**. *The ancient Greeks had a frugal diet and ate mostly wheat, olive oil, and wine* is an independent clause that stands on its own and *they managed to make the most of agricultural hardship by creating varied meals with these three staples* is also a complete sentence.

(B)   remember it is okay to start a sentence with "because." The insertion of "because" changes the first phrase into a dependent clause and fixes the run-on error.

(C)   has a "being" so let's not even bother.

(D)   the insertion of the second "and" creates a sentence fragment.

(E)   they give us the extra pronoun "them," which is as offensive as inserting an "it" into the sentence.

Revised sentence:

<u>Because the ancient Greeks had a frugal diet made</u>
<u>up of mostly wheat, olive oil, and wine, they</u> managed
to make the most of agricultural hardship by
creating varied meals with these three staples.

Correct Answer: (B)

12. The Scripps National Spelling Bee attracts
    students <u>having mastered</u> words that the majority
    of adults do not yet know how to spell, such as
    menhir and apodyterium.

    (A) having mastered
    (B) for mastering
    (C) who have mastered
    (D) to be mastering
    (E) and they mastered

90

"having mastered" is an **Awkward "ing."** A general rule of thumb is to stay away from the words *having* and *being*.

(B)   "for mastering" is another awkward "ing" that does nothing to fix the error.
(C)   "attracts students who have mastered" fixes the awkward "ing" and the sentence is clearer and less wordy.
(D)   "attracts students to be mastering" makes no sense.
(E)   inserts a "they." Stay away from ambiguous pronouns!

Revised sentence:

The Scripps National Spelling Bee attracts students <u>who have mastered</u> words that the majority of adults do not yet know how to spell, such as menhir and apodyterium.

Correct Answer: (C)

13. Although he wrote over 2500 years ago, the Greek playwright Sophocles is still being <u>read, his plays are</u> performed on stages all over the world.

(A)   read, his plays are
(B)   read; his plays being
(C)   read: his plays are being
(D)   read; his plays are
(E)   read, yet his plays are

The sentence as written is a **Run-on.** *Although he wrote over 2500 years ago, the Greek playwright Sophocles is still being read* is an independent clause that stands on its own, and *his plays are performed on stages all over the world* is also an independent clause.

(B)   there is a "being" in the part of the sentence that is not underlined. We can't do anything about that, but we most definitely don't want to add another "being" to the mix! Also, his *plays being performed* sets up a dependent clause so shouldn't be prefaced by a semi-colon.
(C)   "being" is bad.
(D)   the semi-colon takes care of the run-on error.
(E)   "yet" changes the direction of the sentence. We don't have two opposing ideas; the fact that *Sophocles is still read* and *his plays are still performed* fall in line with each other.

Revised sentence:

Although he wrote over 2500 years ago, the Greek playwright Sophocles is still being <u>read; his plays are</u> performed on stages all over the world.

Correct Answer: (D)

14. When walking down the aisle, <u>not stepping on her</u> <u>train and tripping should be the bride's primary</u> <u>concern.</u>

    (A) not stepping on her train and tripping should
          be the bride's primary concern
    (B) not stepping on her train and tripping should
          be what primarily concerns the bride
    (C) the train and not tripping on it should be the
          bride's primary concern
    (D) the bride should be primarily concerned with
          not stepping on her train and tripping
    (E) the bride, regarding not stepping on her train
          and tripping, should be primarily concerned

Notice the intro "ing" phrase followed by a comma (*When walking down the aisle*) to help you catch the **Misplaced Modifier** error. Remember that whatever immediately follows the modifying phrase is what's being modified. According to the sentence as written, *not stepping on her train* is what is *walking down the aisle*.

    (B)   *not stepping on her train* is what is walking down the aisle in this answer choice too.
    (C)   here we have *the train and not tripping on it* walking down the aisle.
    (D)   *the bride* is walking down the aisle, fixing the misplaced modifier issue.
    (E)   although the misplaced modifier error is fixed, this answer choice brings in a slew of other problems and is just plain wordy.

Revised sentence:

When walking down the aisle, <u>the bride should be</u> <u>primarily concerned with not stepping on her train</u> <u>and tripping.</u>

Correct Answer: (D)

15. A severe case of pneumonia suddenly hit Rachel
    on her birthday, February 12th, preventing her
    from attending her own birthday party in the
    <u>evening, the guests were not warned because</u>
    <u>of Rachel being so sick.</u>

    (A) evening, the guests were not warned because
          of Rachel being so sick
    (B) evening; not warning the guests because
          Rachel was so sick
    (C) evening, because Rachel was so sick, the
          guests were not warned
    (D) evening; the guests were not warned because
          Rachel was so sick
    (E) evening and not warning the guests, which
          was caused by Rachel being so sick

Check out the comma followed by the article "the." It's a **Run-on** error. There is a "being"!

(B)   a semi-colon functions like a period. It separates two independent clauses. *Not warning the guests because Rachel was so sick*, is not a complete sentence, so it can't be separated from the first phrase with a semi-colon.

(C)   *A severe case of pneumonia hit Rachel on her birthday, February 12th, preventing her from attending her own birthday party in the evening* is an independent clause and *because Rachel was so sick, the guests were not warned* is also an independent clause. Two independent clauses cannot be separated by just a comma. We need an additional conjunction.

(D)   the semi-colon correctly separates the two independent clauses: *A severe case of pneumonia hit Rachel on her birthday, February 12th, preventing her from attending her own birthday party in the evening* and *the guests were not warned because Rachel was so sick.*

(E)   it has a "being" and is way too wordy and wrong.

Revised sentence:

A severe case of pneumonia suddenly hit Rachel on her birthday, February 12th, preventing her from attending her own birthday party in the evening; the guests were not warned because Rachel was so sick.

Correct Answer: (D)

Error ID
Mishmash Drill

1. <u>While working</u> in Tanzania studying chimpanzees,
     A

Jane Goodall <u>becoming</u> one of the first primatologists
         B

<u>to observe</u> the aggressive nature of these primates
  C

<u>with her</u> discovery that some female chimps kill and
  D

sometimes eat the young of other females to assert

their dominance. <u>No error</u>
          E

2. Ayn Rand, a Russian-born <u>immigrant</u> to the United
                 A

States and a popular author <u>in the genre</u> of fiction,
                 B

<u>who expressed</u> the philosophy of Objectivism <u>in</u>
    C   D

her writings. <u>No error</u>
        E

3. <u>Over the last</u> decade, ACEA members <u>have</u>
   A   B

implemented more than 50 new, CO2 cutting

technologies into their vehicles to <u>reducing</u>
                       C

CO2 emissions <u>for improved</u> fuel efficiency.
            D

<u>No error</u>
  E

4. The <u>most effective</u> acting teachers do not have
       A

<u>their</u> students merely practice techniques and vocal
  B

exercises; they <u>make sure that</u> their students also
          C

<u>utilize</u> sense memory and imagination. <u>No error</u>
  D   E

5. Fitness experts generally <u>seem to find</u> yoga the
                 A   B

<u>more</u> comprehensive <u>of</u> three common exercise
  C   D

programs for weight loss and strength building.

<u>No error</u>
 E

6. According to last week's Nielson ratings, most

viewers <u>were disappointed by</u> the <u>networks</u>' inability
         A   B

<u>developing</u> original reality <u>shows on</u> meaningful
  C   D

topics. <u>No error</u>
     E

7. <u>Rushing through</u> the wind chimes, today's morning
   A

gale <u>chimed</u> <u>more louder</u> jingles <u>as</u> it passed by our
     B   C   D

house. <u>No error</u>
     E

8. <u>After</u> working for a few years in a corporate job,
   A

the young <u>woman decided</u> that working at a small
         B

boutique firm <u>was better</u> than <u>a large corporation</u>.
        C   D

<u>No error</u>
  E

9. <u>As</u> adults, social wasps <u>live not</u> in nests of
  A   B

<u>their own</u> making but rather in nests <u>made by</u>
  C   D

the queen. <u>No error</u>
       E

10. Those entrepreneurs <u>who</u> <u>started</u> dot coms just
            A   B

as the Internet boomed in the early 1990s were

<u>either</u> wise or <u>extraordinary</u> lucky. <u>No error</u>
  C   D   E

11. Most of the hexagonal columnar joints of Gilbert

Hill are the remnants of a ridge that <u>no longer</u>
                        A

exists, the result of heavy construction and

urbanization that has <u>negatively</u> <u>affected</u>
             B   C

<u>the hill's</u> surrounding area. <u>No error</u>
  D   E

12. Mrs. Ray <u>boastfully</u> presented <u>her son's</u> new
         A   B

invention, <u>a washing machine that dries</u>, fluffs,
             C

and folds when <u>pushing a button</u>. <u>No error</u>
         D   E

13. Most microorganisms are not visible to the naked

eye, although some <u>of them</u> <u>found in</u> the ocean
              A   B

sediments of the continental shelf of Namibia

<u>are visible</u> <u>as</u> thin strings of pearls. <u>No error</u>
  C   D   E

14. At a time <u>when</u> appreciation for the trends of the
       A

eighties <u>seems</u> on the verge <u>to vanish</u>, clothing
       B   C

styles such as leg warmers and fanny packs <u>manage</u>
                            D

to enjoy a resurgence of popularity. <u>No error</u>
                       E

15. <u>During</u> the 14th century, classical antiquity gained
  A

renewed importance <u>when both</u> writers and artists
              B

<u>turned to</u> ancient Greek culture <u>for</u> inspiration.
  C   D

<u>No error</u>
  E

16. <u>Although</u> she wasn't happy, Ashley <u>hadn't</u> cried
  A   B

but once <u>during</u> the <u>last</u> two weeks. <u>No error</u>
      C   D   E

17. An effective <u>advocate to</u> non-violence, Mahatma
          A

Gandhi <u>launched</u> several famous hunger strikes
      B

<u>to protest</u> British rule <u>of India</u>. <u>No error</u>
  C   D   E

18. Constant use of antibiotics to treat infections

<u>both destroys</u> <u>many benign</u> bacteria and <u>encourages</u>
  A   B   C

harmful ones to cultivate <u>even more resistant</u>
                   D

strains. <u>No error</u>
     E

19. She bargained <u>more aggressively,</u> <u>rising</u> the price
                              A   B

she <u>was willing</u> to pay and staying well below
       C

the price she <u>wasn't</u>. <u>No error</u>
               D   E

20. Her daughter <u>is submitting</u> applications <u>to several</u>
                        A   B

scholarship funds <u>in</u> the hope <u>to acquire</u>
                  C   D

financial aid to pay for college. <u>No error</u>
                                E

21. Annual tourists <u>to</u> Hawaii's Oahu Island <u>number</u>
                     A   B

<u>almost</u> three times <u>that of Hawaii's Big Island</u>.
   C   D

<u>No error</u>
   E

22. In the socialist society <u>created by</u> George Orwell in
                            A

Animal Farm, both Snowball and Napoleon appear

<u>early on</u> as <u>the leader</u> <u>of</u> the animals. <u>No error</u>
   B   C   D   E

23. <u>Most of</u> the <u>hypotheses that</u> Galileo developed to
     A   B

explain the relationship between the Earth and the

Sun were <u>declared</u> <u>inconsistent to</u> the heliocentric
            C   D

view. <u>No error</u>
       E

24. George Herbert Mead's theory <u>that</u> the emergence
                              A

of the mind and self is a social process <u>involving</u>
                              B

communication rather than individual experience

<u>differs</u> dramatically from <u>most philosophers</u> of his time.
  C   D

<u>No error</u>
   E

25. A nonprofit organization, Project Angel Food

<u>has been serving</u> needy people <u>since</u> 1989,
        A   B

annually delivering <u>nearly</u> 700,000 meals
                    C

<u>each year</u>. <u>No error</u>
   D   E

Answers and Explanations

1. <u>While working</u> in Tanzania studying chimpanzees,
       A

   Jane Goodall <u>becoming</u> one of the first primatologists
            B

   <u>to observe</u> the aggressive nature of these primates
      C

   <u>with her</u> discovery that some female chimps kill and
      D

   sometimes eat the young of other females to assert

   their dominance. <u>No error</u>
              E

If you read the sentence in its entirety you will hopefully hear the **Sentence Fragment** error created by the awkward "ing" (becoming) in answer choice (B). Let's check each of the underlined portions one by one.

(A)   "while working" - We have a gerund, so let's check to see if we should make it an infinitive (to work). Nope. That would change the meaning and grammatically wouldn't work with the rest of the sentence. I would also make sure the "while" isn't setting up a misplaced modifier. The phrase modifies *Jane Goodall*, so all is well.

(B)   "becoming" is a gerund, so let's check to see if we should make it an infinitive (to become). That doesn't work grammatically, so let's change the tense to simple past (became). Now that works MUCH better and corrects the sentence fragment error. *She BECAME while she was working.*

(C)   "to observe" is an infinitive so we should check to see if it should be a gerund (observing). Nope. That would make the sentence fragment error even worse.

(D)   "with her." Let's first check the preposition "with." Can you *observe with*? Sure! After all, you can *observe the stars with a telescope*. Now let's check the pronoun "her." "Her" is a possessive pronoun and the *discovery* belongs to *her*, so that checks fine.

Revised sentence:

While working in Tanzania studying chimpanzees,

A   *became*

Jane Goodall ~~becoming~~ one of the first primatologists

(B)

to observe the aggressive nature of these primates

C

with her discovery that female chimps will kill and

D

sometimes eat the young of other females to assert

their dominance. No error

E

Sentence Fragment / Tense

Correct Answer: (B)

2. Ayn Rand, a Russian-born immigrant to the United

A

States and a popular author in the genre of fiction,

B

who expressed the philosophy of Objectivism in

C   D

her writings. No error

E

We have another **Sentence Fragment** error. But what is causing the problem?

(A) "immigrant" is a noun, and ETS is testing diction. Should it be "emigrant"? No. *immigrant* is someone who comes INTO a country, and *emigrant* is someone who EXITS a country.

(B) is "in" the correct preposition? *Author in the genre of…* works fine.

(C) Once you have checked the underlined portions of the phrase between the two commas, ELIMINATE it, as it is there to distract you. If you cross out *a Russian-born immigrant to the United States and a popular author in the genre of fiction* the sentence reads – *Ayn Rand who founded the philosophy of Objectivism in her writings.* This is not a complete sentence. Remove the "who" – *Ayn Rand founded the philosophy of Objectivism in her writings.* That's the fix we want!

(D) Cross out the prep phrase *of objectivism* to test the preposition "in." Make a sentence on your own, like: *Plato espoused his philosophy in his writings.* Checks out fine!

Revised sentence:

Ayn Rand, a Russian-born immigrant to the United

A

States and a popular author in the genre of fiction,

B

~~who~~ expressed the philosophy of Objectivism in

(C)   D

her writings. No error.

E

Sentence Fragment

Correct Answer: (C)

98

3. <u>Over the last</u> decade, ACEA members <u>have</u>
       A   B

implemented more than 50 new, CO_2 cutting

technologies into their vehicles to <u>reducing</u>
                                           C

CO_2 emissions <u>for improved</u> fuel efficiency.
                                   D

<u>No error</u>
   E

Your ear might easily catch this one. It's those nasty **Gerunds** once again.

(A)   "over" is a preposition. Is *over the last decade* a legitimate prep phrase? Yes, it is.

(B)   "have" is not simply a present tense verb. It is linked to *implemented* (have implemented). Let's test present perfect tense. See the clue word "over." We have an action that has floated in the past at no set time, so present perfect tense is correct. Be sure to also check for SVA. *Who* or *what* "have implemented"? *Members*. Plural verb, plural subject checks.

(C)   "reducing" is a gerund, but it is connected to the word "to." Infinitives should be connected to "to," not gerunds. Change *reducing* to *reduce*.

(D)   test the preposition "for," by simplifying the sentence. *To reduce emissions for improved efficiency*. That checks fine.

Revised sentence:

<u>Over the last decade</u>, ACEA members <u>have</u>
     A   B
implemented more than 50 new, CO_2 cutting

                         reduce   *Gerund / Infinitive Switch*
technologies into their vehicles to ~~reducing~~
                                      Ⓒ

CO_2 emissions <u>for improved</u> fuel efficiency.
                                   D

<u>No error</u>
   E

Correct Answer: (C)

4. The <u>most effective</u> acting teachers do not have
          A

   <u>their</u> students merely practice techniques and vocal
     B

   exercises; they <u>make sure that</u> their students also
                        C

   <u>utilize</u> sense memory and imagination. <u>No error</u>
     D   E

You hopefully didn't catch anything glaringly wrong on a first read of the sentence. It is always helpful, however, to check each answer choice to make sure you didn't miss anything.

   (A)   we have to make sure "most" refers to three or more things. There are more than three acting teachers in the world so "most" checks out fine. "Effective" is an adjective modifying "teachers" (a noun) so that works too.
   (B)   first let's make sure "their" is not ambiguous. It can only refer to acting teachers and both the pronoun and its antecedent are plural so there is no pronoun agreement error. "Their" is a possessive pronoun and the *students* belong to the *teachers*, so pronoun case is correct as well.
   (C)   "make" is a present tense verb, and the sentence is occurring in the present as evidenced by the verbs "do" and "practice." "They" is plural and "make" is plural so SVA works. Is the preposition "that" correct? Yes. I'm sure you've all heard the expression *make sure that you lock the door.*
   (D)   "utilize" is a present tense verb. We've already established that the sentence takes place in the present so verb tense works. Check for SVA. *Who* or *what* "utilize"? *Students.* "Students" is plural as is "utilize" so SVA checks fine.

Correct Answer: (E)

5. Fitness experts generally <u>seem</u> <u>to find</u> yoga the
                               A   B

   <u>more</u> comprehensive <u>of</u> three common exercise
     C   D

   programs for weight loss and strength building.

   <u>No error</u>
      E

We have a **Counting** error. Let's check the answer choices one by one.

   (A)   "seem" is a present tense verb. Are we in the present? Yes! Let's check for SVA. *Who* or *what* "seem to find"? *Fitness experts.* "Experts" is plural as is "seem" so SVA checks.
   (B)   "to find" is the infinitive. Should it be the gerund (finding) instead? Nope.
   (C)   "more" is a counting word, so we have to see how many things the "more" is comparing. *THREE exercise programs*, so the *more* should be changed to *most*.
   (D)   "of three common exercise programs" is idiomatically correct.

Revised sentence:

Fitness experts generally <u>seem</u> <u>to find</u> yoga the
                              A   B
most
~~more~~ comprehensive <u>of</u> three common exercise
Ⓒ   D

programs for weight loss and strength building.

Counting Error

<u>No error</u>
  E

Correct Answer: (C)

6. According to last week's Nielson ratings, most

   viewers <u>were disappointed by</u> the <u>networks</u>' inability
                   A   B
   <u>developing</u> original reality <u>shows on</u> meaningful
     C   D
   topics. <u>No error</u>
          E

Let's check the answers one by one to catch the **Gerund/Infinitive Switch**.

(A)   let's check SVA for the past tense verb "were." *Who* or *what* "were"? *Viewers*. "Viewers" is plural and "were" is plural so that checks. Let's check the preposition "by." Can you be *disappointed by* someone or something? It happens all the time.

(B)   punctuation is rarely tested, but it looks like we have to check it here. There is more than one *network*, so the apostrophe should indeed follow the "s."

(C)   "developing" is a gerund. Let's check to see if it should be the infinitive "to develop." Make your own sentence. *He was disappointed by her inability TO SING.* That works much better!

(D)   let's test the preposition "on." Can a network develop a show ON something? Sure – *the network developed a show on gorillas.*

Revised sentence:

According to last week's Nielson ratings, most

viewers <u>were disappointed by</u> the <u>networks</u>' inability
to develop   A   B
~~developing~~ original reality <u>shows on</u> meaningful
    Ⓒ   D
topics. <u>No error</u>
       E

Gerund / Infinitive Switch

Correct Answer: (C)

7. <u>Rushing through</u> the wind chimes, today's morning
         A

gale <u>chimed</u> <u>more louder</u> jingles <u>as</u> it passed by our
         B   C   D

house. <u>No error</u>
              E

Your ear might catch this one right away. We have a **Redundancy Error** caused by an **Absolute Word.**

   (A)   "rushing through the wind chimes" is a modifying phrase that is modifying *today's morning gale*. That checks fine. Also check the preposition "through." Can you rush *THROUGH* something? Yes. *He rushed through the crowds.*

   (B)   "chimed" is a simple past tense verb. The sentence is occurring at a specific time in the past (the morning) so it checks out fine.

   (C)   "more louder" violates a grammar rule. You can't modify an "er" word (louder) with "more." Remove the "more" and change to the adjective *loud*, which correctly modifies the noun *jingles*.

   (D)   "as" is a preposition. *chimed as it passed.* That is correct.

Revised sentence:

<u>Rushing through</u> the wind chimes, today's morning
         A   *loud*   *Redundancy / Absolute Word*

gale <u>chimed</u> ~~more louder~~ jingles <u>as</u> it passed by our
         B   Ⓒ   D

house. <u>No error</u>
              E

Correct Answer: (C)

8. <u>After</u> working for a few years in a corporate job,
      A

the young <u>woman decided</u> that working at a small
                    B

boutique firm <u>was better</u> than <u>a large corporation</u>.
                    C   D

<u>No error</u>
      E

Unclear Comparisons are sometimes difficult to spot in a first read. Let's check one by one.

   (A)   we have an introductory phrase modifying the young woman, so that checks. Can the young woman decide *AFTER* working? Yes.

   (B)   "decided" is a simple past tense verb and we are in a specific time in the past, so that checks.

   (C)   "was" is a past tense verb and we've already established we are in the past. Check SVA. *What* "was better"? *Working*, which is singular, so SVA checks.

   (D)   Notice the "than" right before "a large corporation." This tips us off to a possible comparison error. What two things are being compared? *Working at a small boutique firm* is being compared to *a large corporation*, when it should be compared to *WORKING at a large corporation*. We have an unclear comparison.

Revised sentence:

<u>After</u> working for a few years in a corporate job,
   A

the young <u>woman decided</u> that working at a small
               B   *working at a large corporation*   *Unclear Comparison*

boutique firm <u>was better</u> than <u>a large corporation</u>.
           C   (D)

<u>No error</u>
  E

Correct Answer: (D)

9. <u>As</u> adults, social wasps <u>live not</u> in nests of
  A   B

  <u>their own</u> making but rather in nests <u>made by</u>
     C   D

  the queen. <u>No error</u>
           E

Seems okay, but go through the answers just in case.

(A)   "as" is a preposition. It might be helpful to simplify and flip flop the sentence to test the preposition. *Social wasps don't live in nests as adults.* That works.

(B)   "live not." Yes, it does sound a bit weird, but it's fine. It translates to, "do not live." It's just a fancier way to say it.

(C)   "their" is a pronoun. First check for ambiguity. "Their" refers to "wasps," so that works, and wasps is plural, so pronoun agreement works, and the "nests" belong to them, so "their" is correctly a possessive pronoun.

(D)   Check the preposition "by." *The meal was made by the cook.* It's passive, but grammatically correct.

Correct Answer: (E)

10. Those entrepreneurs <u>who</u> <u>started</u> dot coms just
                      A   B

    as the Internet boomed in the early 1990s were

    <u>either</u> wise or <u>extraordinary</u> lucky. <u>No error</u>
     C   D   E

This one's an easy fix if you can spot the error! We have an **Adjective/Adverb Error**.

(A)   "who" is a pronoun that refers to "entrepreneurs" so that checks fine.

(B)   "started" is a past tense verb. The sentence refers to the early 1990s, so we are in the past.

(C)   when we see "either" we want to check to make sure there is an "or." Yes, we have an *either/or* set up.

(D)   "extraordinary" is an adjective so we need to make sure it isn't supposed to be an adverb. What is it modifying? The adjective "lucky." Adjectives don't modify adjectives, so we need to make *extraordinary* an adverb, *extraordinarily*.

Revised sentence:

Those entrepreneurs <u>who</u> <u>started</u> dot coms just
                A   B

as the Internet boomed in the early 1990s were
         extraordinarily   *Adjective / Adverb*

<u>either</u> wise or ~~<u>extraordinary</u>~~ lucky.
  C   Ⓓ

<u>No error</u>
   E

Correct Answer: (D)

11. Most of the hexagonal columnar joints of Gilbert

Hill are the remnants of a ridge that <u>no longer</u>
                                  A

exists, the result of heavy construction and

urbanization that has <u>negatively</u> <u>affected</u>
                     B   C

<u>the hill's</u> surrounding area. <u>No error</u>
   D   E

Let's check the answer choices one by one to make sure that we are not missing an error.

- (A)   check the phrase "no longer." Can something *no longer* exist? Sure. *Her belief in true love no longer exists.*
- (B)   "negatively" is an adverb that modifies the verb "affected."
- (C)   "affected" is a present perfect tense verb. Notice it is connected to "has" - *has affected*. The construction and urbanization occurred in the past and as a result of these past actions the *remnants* no longer exist in the present, so verb tense is correct. ETS is also testing the diction of "affected" against the similarly spelled word "effected." ETS will use "affect" as a verb (to affect something – meaning "to influence") and "effect" as a noun (the result of something).
- (D)   "the hill's" is the region we are talking about. Let's check the punctuation. *Hill* is singular so it should indeed be attached to an apostrophe followed by an "s."

Correct Answer: (E)

12. Mrs. Ray <u>boastfully</u> presented <u>her son's</u> new
              A   B

   invention, <u>a washing machine that dries</u>, fluffs,
                           C

   and folds when <u>pushing a button</u>. <u>No error</u>
                   D   E

Did you laugh out loud when you read the sentence, or did you miss the **Misplaced Modifier** error?

- (A)   "boastfully" is an adverb modifying the way she "presented" the invention. Adverbs modify verbs so it checks.

(B)   The son belongs to "her" and the "invention" belongs to the son, so both the possessive pronoun (her) and the possessive apostrophe (son's) work.

(C)   *a washing machine that dries…* is a dependent clause and should be preceded by a comma. "dries" is a singular verb and "washing machine" is its singular subject. *Dries* is also parallel to *fluffs* and *folds*.

(D)   according to the sentence as written, *who* or *what* is "pushing the button"? The *washing machine!* Oops. That can't be right.

Revised sentence:

Mrs. Ray boastfully presented her son's new
               A   B

Misplaced Modifier

invention, a washing machine that dries,
                 C   *a button is pushed OR you push a button*

fluffs, and folds when ~~pushing a button~~.
                 (D)

No error
   E

Correct Answer: (D)

13. Most microorganisms are not visible to the naked

eye, although some of them found in the ocean
                      A   B

sediments of the continental shelf of Namibia

are visible as thin strings of pearls. No error
   C   D   E

Let's check the answers one by one to be on the safe side.

(A)   check the preposition "of." Make a new expression – *some of the boys…* That works. Let's check for pronoun ambiguity. Who does "them" refer to? *Microorganisms.* It's the only plural noun in the first part of the sentence, so the reference is clear. Both the pronoun and the noun it refers to are plural, so pronoun agreement checks fine. The preposition "of" comes before the pronoun "them" so the objective case is also correct.

(B)   can "microorganisms" be *found in* the ocean? Yes.

(C)   Let's check the simple present tense verb "are" for SVA. *Who* or *what* "are"? Be sure to eliminate the following prep phrases: *to the naked eye, of them, in the ocean sediments, of the continental shelf, of Namibia.* The sentence then reads: *Most microorganisms are not visible, although some found are visible…* the "are" refers to "microorganisms."

(D)   "as" is a preposition. Can something be *visible as?* Yes. *Chromosomes are not visible as separate units.*

Correct Answer: (E)

14. At a time <u>when</u> appreciation for the trends of the
            A

  eighties <u>seems</u> on the verge <u>to vanish</u>, clothing
         B   C

  styles such as leg warmers and fanny packs <u>manage</u>
                                         D

  to enjoy a resurgence of popularity. <u>No error</u>
                                    E

Your ear might have caught the **Gerund/Infinitive Switch**, but let's go through each of the answer choices.

(A)   "when" refers to time, so that checks.

(B)   "seems" is a simple present tense verb so let's check for SVA. *Who* or *what* "seems"? Cross out the prep phrases *for the trends* and *of the eighties*. The sentence now reads – *At a time when appreciation seems…* "appreciation" is singular as is "seems" so SVA checks.

(C)   "to vanish" is an infinitive so let's check to see if it should be a gerund (of vanishing) instead. *appreciation seems on the verge of vanishing*. Much better!

(D)   "manage" is a simple present tense verb. *Who* or *what* "manage"? *Leg warmers* AND *fanny packs*. Plural subject and plural verb match.

Revised sentence:

At a time <u>when</u> appreciation for the trends of the
         A   *of vanishing*   *Gerund / Infinitive Switch*

eighties <u>seems</u> on the verge <u>to ~~vanish~~</u>, clothing
      B   Ⓒ

styles such as leg warmers and fanny packs <u>manage</u>
                                     D

to enjoy a resurgence of popularity. <u>No error</u>
                                E

Correct Answer: (C)

15. <u>During</u> the 14th century, classical antiquity gained
     A

  renewed importance <u>when both</u> writers and artists
                      B

  <u>turned to</u> ancient Greek culture <u>for</u> inspiration.
     C   D

  <u>No error</u>
    E

Didn't spot an error on the first read through? Let's check the answers one by one.

(A)   is "during" the correct preposition? Make your own sentence. *During the dance…* It works!

(B)   "when" refers to time and the sentence is set in the 14th century, so "when" is correct. "both" tells us to check and make sure there is an "and." Yes. *Both writers AND artists*.

(C)   "turned" is a past tense verb, and we've already established that the sentence is set in the past (14th century). Check the preposition "to." Make your own sentence – *She turned to her friend for comfort*. It's fine as is.

(D)   check the preposition "for." Can you *turn to something for inspiration?* Absolutely.

Correct Answer: (E)

16. <u>Although</u> she wasn't happy, Ashley <u>hadn't</u> cried
     A   B
    but once <u>during</u> the <u>last</u> two weeks. <u>No error</u>
               C   D   E

This **Double Negative** error is not as easy to catch as some of the others.

(A)   "although" is a conjunction that flips the direction of the sentence. *Not being happy* and *not crying* are opposites, so the "although" works. Or think of it without the nots. If someone is sad, it is typical to cry. Ashley has only cried once, so we have an opposite relationship.

(B)   separate the "hadn't" into "had not." *Ashley had not cried but once.* We have a "not" and a "but," creating a double negative. The sentence should read: *Ashley had cried but once.*

(C)   is "during" the correct preposition? Make your own sentence: *I sleep during the night.* Works for me.

(D)   "last" is an adverb modifying the adjective "two" and is therefore correct.

Revised sentence:

                                 had   *Double Negative*

Although she wasn't happy, Ashley ~~hadn't~~ cried
  A   Ⓑ
but once <u>during</u> the <u>last</u> two weeks. <u>No error</u>
         C   D   E

Correct Answer: (B)

17. An effective <u>advocate to</u> non-violence, Mahatma
                   A
    Gandhi <u>launched</u> several famous hunger strikes
            B
    <u>to protest</u> British rule <u>of India</u>. <u>No error</u>
      C   D   E

Did your ear catch the **Idiom** error?

(A)   Can you be an *advocate to* something? NO! You are an *advocate of* something.

(B)   "launched" is a past tense verb. The sentence is set in the past, so it checks fine.

(C)   "to protest" is an infinitive so let's check to see if it should be a gerund (protesting) instead. Nope. That would indicate that the *hunger strikes are protesting* and changes the intended meaning of the sentence.

(D)   "of" is a preposition. Make a new phrase: *rule of thumb.* It works!

Revised sentence:

An effective <u>advocate t̶o̶</u> ~~of~~ non-violence, Mahatma   *Idiom*
                (A)

Gandhi <u>launched</u> several famous hunger strikes
        B

<u>to protest</u> British rule <u>of India</u>. <u>No error</u>
   C   D   E

Correct Answer: (A)

18. Constant use of antibiotics to treat infections

   <u>both destroys</u> <u>many benign</u> bacteria and <u>encourages</u>
     A   B   C

   harmful ones to cultivate <u>even more resistant</u>
                              D

   strains. <u>No error</u>
         E

Nothing should stand out as wrong, but let's work through each answer choice.

    (A)   "both" needs to have an "and" and it does: *both destroys* AND *encourages*. Let's check SVA with the simple present tense verb "destroys." *Who* or *what* "destroys"? The *constant use*. Remember to cross out the prep phrase *of antibiotics*. Singular verb (destroys) singular subject (use) is a match.
    (B)   "many" is an adverb modifying the adjective "benign" which is modifying the noun "bacteria."
    (C)   "encourages" is a simple present tense verb that also refers to "the use," which is singular, so SVA checks out fine.
    (D)   "even" is an adverb modifying "more," which is an adverb modifying the adjective "resistant," which modifies the noun "strains." All good.

Correct Answer: (E)

19. She bargained <u>more aggressively</u>, <u>rising</u> the price
                          A   B

    she <u>was willing</u> to pay and staying well below
               C

    the price she <u>wasn't</u>. <u>No error</u>
                   D   E

Diction errors are some of the most difficult to catch! Check the answers one by one.

- (A) "more" is an adverb modifying the adverb "aggressively," which is modifying the verb "bargained." All is good.
- (B) Can you *"rise" the price of something?* No, but you can *"raise" the price of something.* Tricky!
- (C) "was willing" is a past tense verb. We are in the past, as evidenced by the past tense verb "bargained."
- (D) "wasn't" is parallel to "was willing."

Revised sentence: *raising*   *Diction*

She bargained <u>more aggressively</u>, <s>rising</s> the price
             A   Ⓑ

she <u>was willing</u> to pay and staying well below
       C

the price she <u>wasn't</u>. <u>No error</u>
          D   E

Correct Answer: (B)

20. Her daughter <u>is submitting</u> applications <u>to several</u>
                 A   B

    scholarship funds <u>in</u> the hope <u>to acquire</u>
                 C   D

    financial aid to pay for college. <u>No error</u>
                           E

Go through the answer choices if you didn't catch the **Gerund Infinitive Switch** on the first read.

- (A) first check SVA. "Is" is singular and "daughter" is singular so that checks. She is *in the process of submitting* so the present progressive tense is correct as well.
- (B) Check the preposition "to." Can you *submit to?* Sure – *She submitted her short stories to agents.* "Several" is an adjective that modifies "funds" so that is correct.
- (C) "in the hope," is idiomatically correct.
- (D) "to acquire" is an infinitive so check to see if it should be a gerund (of acquiring) instead - *in the hope of acquiring.* Much better!

Revised sentence:

Her daughter <u>is submitting</u> applications <u>to several</u>
             A   B   *of acquiring*   *Gerund / Infinitive Switch*
scholarship funds <u>in</u> the hope <u>to acquire</u>
             C   Ⓓ
financial aid to pay for college. <u>No error</u>
                               E

Correct Answer: (D)

21. Annual tourists <u>to</u> Hawaii's Oahu Island <u>number</u>
                    A   B
   <u>almost</u> three times <u>that of Hawaii's Big Island</u>.
      C   D
   <u>No error</u>
      E

The **Pronoun Agreement** error is hard to catch.

    (A)   "to" is a preposition. Can you be a *tourist to* somewhere? Yes indeed.
    (B)   "number" is a counting word, so let's check to make sure it shouldn't be "amount." You can count *tourists* so "number" is correct.
    (C)   "almost" is an adverb modifying "three times." Checks out fine.
    (D)   "that of" refers to *tourists*. "Tourists" is plural so change *that* to *those*.

Revised sentence:

Annual tourists <u>to</u> Hawaii's Oahu Island <u>number</u>
                  A   *those*   B   *Pronoun Agreement*
<u>almost</u> three times <u>that of Hawaii's Big Island</u>.
   C   Ⓓ
<u>No error</u>
   E

Correct Answer: (D)

22. In the socialist society <u>created by</u> George Orwell in
A

Animal Farm, both Snowball and Napoleon appear

<u>early on</u> as <u>the leader</u> <u>of</u> the animals. <u>No error</u>
  B   C   D   E

Check the answers one by one to catch the **Noun Agreement** error.

(A) check the preposition "by." Make your own sentence: *The plan was created by her*. That works. "Created" is a past tense verb. George Orwell wrote the book in the past, so verb tense checks fine.

(B) can someone or something *appear early on* in a book? Absolutely.

(C) "leader" is a singular noun so check for noun agreement. Who or what does "leader" refer to? *Napoleon* AND *Snowball*. Two pigs mean two leaders. We have a noun agreement error.

(D) check the preposition "of." Can you be a *leader of* something? Sure – think of the expression *leader of the pack*.

Revised sentence:

In the socialist society <u>created by</u> George Orwell in
A

Animal Farm, both Snowball and Napoleon appear

leaders   *Noun Agreement*

<u>early on</u> as <u>the leader</u> of the animals. <u>No error</u>
  B   Ⓒ   D   E

Correct Answer: (C)

23. <u>Most of</u> the <u>hypotheses that</u> Galileo developed to
    A   B

explain the relationship between the Earth and the

Sun were <u>declared</u> <u>inconsistent to</u> the heliocentric
             C   D

view. <u>No error</u>
       E

Did you catch the **Idiom** error? Let's check the answers.

(A) Should "most" be "more"? No. It is safe to assume that there are more than two hypotheses. Make your own sentence to check the preposition "of." *Most of the dogs...* It works.

(B) "hypotheses that" is idiomatically correct.

(C) "declared" is a past tense verb and Galileo is long since dead and gone, so "declared" checks fine.

(D) Check the preposition "inconsistent to." Make your own sentence: *His actions are inconsistent to his words*? Nope. It should be: *His actions are inconsistent with his words*.

Revised sentence:

Most of the hypotheses that Galileo developed to
  A   B

explain the relationship between the Earth and the
                      with   *Idiom*

Sun were declared inconsistent ~~to~~ the heliocentric view.
       C   (D)

No error
 E

Correct Answer: (D)

24. George Herbert Mead's theory that the emergence
                        A

of the mind and self is a social process involving
                               B

communication rather than individual experience

differs dramatically from most philosophers of his time.
 C   D

No error
 E

Unclear Comparisons are one of the most difficult errors to catch. Did you notice the "differs from"?

(A)   "that" is idiomatically correct. Make your own sentence. *Susie came up with the theory that all boys are dumb.*

(B)   should "involving" (a gerund) be "to involve" (an infinitive)? No.

(C)   check SVA. *Who* or *what* "differs"? Cross out the distracting "that" phrase *that the emergence of the mind and self is a social process involving communication rather than individual experience* and we see that the "theory differs." Singular subject and singular verb checks.

(D)   here is where the comparison error comes into play. The sentence as written is comparing *Mead's theory* to *philosophers*, when it should be comparing *Mead's theory* to the *THEORIES of OTHER philosophers*.

Revised sentence:

George Herbert Mead's theory that the emergence
                    A

of the mind and self is a social process involving
                         B

communication rather than individual experience
           those of most other philosophers   *Comparisons*

differs dramatically from ~~most philosophers~~ of his time.
 C   (D)

No error
 E

Correct Answer: (D)

112

25. A nonprofit organization, Project Angel Food

has been serving needy people since 1989,
      A   B

annually delivering nearly 700,000 meals
                           C

each year. No error
     D   E

Redundancy errors are extremely hard to catch! Check the answers one by one.

(A)   "has been serving" is a present perfect verb. Is this an action that started in the past and continues on into the present? Yes! *Serving since 1989.*

(B)   "since" is the correct conjunction and appropriately sets up the present perfect tense.

(C)   "nearly" is an adverb modifying the "700,000 meals."

(D)   "each year" is redundant to "annually." Remove it!

Revised sentence:

A nonprofit organization, Project Angel Food

has been serving needy people since 1989,
     A   B

annually delivering nearly 700,000 meals
                        C

~~each year~~. No error   *Redundancy*
    Ⓓ   E

Correct Answer: (D)

Chapter 6
Improving Paragraphs

The *Improving Paragraphs* questions follow the Error Id questions on the 25-minute grammar section of the SAT. They are always questions 30-35. Made up of easy and medium questions...

⟶ **the Improving Paragraphs section should never be left undone.**

Make sure you leave enough time for it, even if that means skipping the more difficult Error ID problems.

What it is: You are being asked to revise a student's rough draft of an essay. Every sentence is numbered. Sometimes you will be asked to refer back to the passage, but often ETS reproduces the sentence below the question.

How to Tackle: Always keep in mind the 19 grammar rules and remember that *clear and concise* is preferred.

⟶ **Step 1: If time allows, read the entire essay. Don't get bogged down by the wordy and incorrect grammar, just read the passage for a sense of the student's main idea and tone. Read it quickly, as you aren't dealing with a reading comprehension passage.**

⟶ **Step 2: Determine if you are on a specific question or a general question.**

Specific questions ask you to revise a sentence or combine two sentences. On specific questions, it is a good idea to read the sentences before and after the given sentence in order to remain true to the context and flow of the passage.

General questions ask you to omit or add a sentence and refer to the passage as a whole. If you have not read the entire essay, you may miss the general questions.

> **On Improving Paragraphs questions, answer choice (A) is not a restatement of the given sentence, unless ETS states *(A) (As it is now)*.**

Tips:

#1 - Conjunctions: When ETS is testing conjunctions you must read the sentence before to test the direction of the given sentence. Ask: *Is it following along the same direction or flipping direction?* You can also use the answer choices to help you out. If you notice that 4 of the answer choices are flipping direction with conjunctions such as *but, although, however,* and *yet,* and there is only one answer choice that keeps it going the same direction, such as *and,* then you know the correct answer is going to be the odd answer choice out (*and*).

#2 - Pronouns: ETS loves to test pronouns (especially pronoun ambiguity) on Improving Paragraphs. When you see a pronoun such as *they, it, this, those,* or *that,* read the surrounding sentences to see what the pronoun refers to. Replace the pronoun with a noun, even if it seems a bit repetitive.

34. In context, which of the following is the best way to revise the underlined portion of sentence 9 (reproduced below)?

    <u>They will be the most important</u> *factor that helps you stand out from the rest of the applicants.*

    (A) (As it is now)
    (B) Participating in them is the most important
    (C) These activities, being done, will be the most important
    (D) Participating in these activities will be the most important
    (E) If you participate in them, it will be the most important

Take a look at the specific section of the passage that this question refers to:

(8) You can be sure that your admittance to college rests on your extracurricular activities. (9) They will be the most important factor that helps you stand out from the rest of the applicants.

Notice the ambiguous pronoun "they." Read sentence 8 to see who or what the "they" refers to. *Extracurricular activities.* What answer choices specify "activities"? (C) and (D), but (C) has a "being" and is way wordy. (D) is the correct answer.

$\longrightarrow$ **Clear, concise, and unambiguous.**

#3 - "ing" words: Avoid those awkward "ing" words, particularly *having* and *being*!

> **If you are running out of time, don't read the essay, rather answer all the specific questions first to avoid leaving too many answer choices blank.**

Let's do an Improving Paragraphs section together.

$\longrightarrow$ **Remember to read the essay first, keeping in mind the main idea!**

(1) Many parents consider video games violent and a waste of time and energy. (2) A recent version of the acclaimed video game *Grand Theft Auto* evoked disparaging reviews from child advocates, they are people who believe that violent games result in aggressive behavior in children and teens. (3) The only affirmative ones expressed relief that the Entertainment Software Rating Board (ESRB) rated the video game Mature. (4) Wouldn't they be forever scarred to play a video game that contained violence, strong language, and sexual content? (5) And *Manhunt 2*, the action/adventure game sequel to Rockstar Games 2003's *Manhunt*. (6) Imagine equating the violence one sees on the big screen with real life.

(7) I see nothing wrong with video games, whether violent or of the *Guitar Hero* variety. (8) After all, aren't Looney Tunes cartoons just as violent? (9) For example, remember the Bugs Bunny episode where Bugs pulls out a gun and shoots an innocent man for coughing? (10) Cartoons would never have become so popular if the gags did not include violence and innuendo. (11) No doubt, video game players recognize the violent actions of modern day video game characters, they are reminiscent of those of classic cartoon characters, such as Wile E. Coyote, created by the late Chuck Jones. (12) Jones will see traces of his characters in the antics of the *Grand Theft Auto* players. (13) Wile E. Coyote blows himself up with Acme Dynamite, and would feel right at home in the world of *Grand Theft Auto*.

(14) Violence has been prevalent in entertainment since the first cartoons, and we should not assume that children and teenagers are unable to differentiate violence for entertainment's sake, from real-life violence.

What is the main idea of the essay? *There is nothing wrong with video games; they are no more violent than Looney Tunes cartoons.*

We are now ready to answer the questions.

30. Which of the following is the best version of the underlined portion of sentence 2 (reproduced below)?

A recent version of the acclaimed video game Grand Theft Auto evoked disparaging reviews from <u>child advocates, they are people who believe</u> that violent games result in aggressive behavior in children and teens.

(A) (As it is now)
(B) child advocates; they were people who believed
(C) child advocates in believing
(D) child advocates. These believed
(E) child advocates, those who believe

Did you notice the run-on created in the given sentence? Spot the visual (*"…advocates, they…"*) *A recent version of the acclaimed video game Grand theft Auto evoked disparaging reviews from child advocates* is an independent clause that stands on its own, and *they are people who believe that violent games result in aggressive behavior in children and teens* is also a complete sentence. We need to add a conjunction after the comma, replace the comma with a semi-colon or period, or turn the second phrase into a dependent clause. Eliminate (A).

(B) inserts a semi-colon, but ETS has switched to past tense, indicating that *child advocates* are no longer part of the present. This changes the intended meaning of the sentence. Careful of those switches in tenses! Eliminate (B).
(C) gives us an awkward "ing" (believing) and is not idiomatically correct. Eliminate (C).
(D) ETS fixes the run-on by inserting a period after "advocates," but creates another problem with the ambiguous pronoun "these." Who the heck is *these*? It also switches tenses. Eliminate (D).
(E) Let's just look at the clause *those who believe that violent games result in aggressive behavior in children and teens.* Is that clause dependent or independent? It is *dependent*, which means it cannot stand on its own and should be connected to the previous phrase with only a comma. (E) is correct.

31. In context, which of the following is the best word to use instead of "ones" in sentence 3?

(A) games
(B) cases
(C) characters
(D) reviews
(E) portions

"Ones" is a pronoun, so we need to read the sentence above sentence 3 to see what the "ones" refers to.

(2) A recent version of the acclaimed video game Grand Theft Auto evoked disparaging reviews from child advocates, they are people who believe that violent games result in aggressive behavior in children and teens. (3) The only affirmative ones expressed relief that the Entertainment Software Rating Board (ESRB) rated the video game Mature.

The "ones" refers to "reviews." Or you can go through the answer choices one by one. Can *games* express relief? No. Can *cases* express relief? No. Can *characters* express relief? In the game itself, yes, but in regards to the *reviews*, no. Can "portions" express relief? No. (D) is the correct answer.

32. In context, which of the following is the best version of the underlined portion of sentence 5 (reproduced below)?

And Manhunt 2, the action/adventure game sequel to Rockstar Games 2003's Manhunt.

(A) (as it is now)
(B) *Manhunt 2* is the
(C) Another supposed outrage is *Manhunt 2*, the
(D) We can also take offense at *Manhunt 2*, the
(E) Yet consider *Manhunt 2*, which is the

Notice those words, "in context." Be sure to read the sentence before as well.

(4) Wouldn't they be forever scarred to play a video game that contained violence, strong language, and sexual content? (5) And Manhunt 2, the action/adventure game sequel to Rockstar Games 2003's Manhunt.

Did you notice that not only is sentence 5 a fragment, but there is also no transition from sentence 4? Eliminate (A).

(B) takes care of the sentence fragment issue, but still doesn't give us a transition, so is probably not going to be the BEST answer.
(C) *Another supposed outrage…* gives us the transition we want and fixes the sentence fragment issue. The correct answer is (C).
(D) *We can also take offense…*provides a transition and fixes the fragment, but goes against the main idea. The author doesn't think video games are offensive, and so wouldn't use the pronoun "we" to include himself in the group of critics.
(E) the "yet" indicates a flip in the direction of the sentence, however, *Manhunt 2* is given as an additional example. The transition should follow along the same direction as the sentence before, not flip the direction.

33. An important tactic used in the first paragraph is to

(A) expand on a perspective that contrasts with the author's argument
(B) use graphic detail to animate a personal experience
(C) provide a well thought out, objective analysis of modern parenting
(D) introduce an unconventional approach to creating video games
(E) reveal the sense of playfulness implicit in much parental concern

This is a general question. Reread the first paragraph to familiarize yourself before looking at the answer choices. Then go through the answer choices one by one.

(A) what *perspective* does the writer *expand on* in this paragraph: *The idea that video games are violent and a bad influence on kids*. The author *disagrees* with this perspective in the subsequent paragraphs. So yes, (A) is probably the right answer. But let's check the others just in case.

(B) the author doesn't get *personal* and there is no *graphic detail*.

(C) The topic of the first paragraph is video games, not *modern parenting*.

(D) The first paragraph is not about *creating* video games. It is about a *particular response* to video games.

(E) The *concern* is not limited to parents, and there is nothing *playful* about that concern.

34. Which of the following is the best version of the underlined portion of sentence 11 (reproduced below)?

No doubt, video game players recognize the violent actions of modern day video game characters, they are *reminiscent of those of classic cartoon characters, such as Wile E. Coyote, created by the late Chuck Jones*.

(A) (as it is now)
(B) characters, they would be
(C) characters; they were
(D) characters for being
(E) characters as

Did you notice the run-on created in the given sentence? Spot the visual ("…*characters, they are*…") *No doubt, video game players recognize the violent actions of modern day video game characters* is an independent clause that stands on its own, and *they are reminiscent of those of classic cartoon characters, such as Wile E. Coyote, created by the late Chuck Jones* is also a complete sentence. We need to add a conjunction after the comma, replace the comma with a semi-colon or period, or turn the second phrase into a dependent clause. Eliminate (A) and (B), which are both run-ons.

(C) fixes the run-on by inserting a semi-colon, but changes the tense to past tense (were). The sentence discusses *modern day video game characters* so we need the present tense. Eliminate (C).

(D) has a "being." Eliminate (D).

(E) can something be *recognized as reminiscent* of something else? Absolutely. (E) fixes the run-on by adding the conjunction "as."

35. In context, which of the following is the best way to revise the underlined portion of sentence 12 (reproduced below)?

Jones will see traces of his characters in the antics of the Grand Theft Auto players.

(A) However, Jones might have seen
(B) Likewise, Jones can see
(C) In addition to this, Jones would see
(D) Jones could have seen
(E) Jones, too, would see

At first glance, it is difficult to spot the error with this sentence. Skim the answer choices, and notice the *however, likewise, in addition to this*, and *too*. Must have something to do with transitions, so let's read sentence 11 as well.

(11) No doubt, video game players recognize the violent actions of modern day video game characters, they are reminiscent of those of classic cartoon characters, such as Wile E. Coyote, created by the late Chuck Jones. (12) Jones will see traces of his characters in the antics of the Grand Theft Auto players.

Ask: *Is sentence 12 going in the same direction as sentence 11 or does it flip direction?* The same! *The characters are reminiscent* is along the same lines as *Jones will see traces of his characters in the antics of Grand Theft Auto players*. So we don't want a conjunction that flips the direction. Eliminate (A).

(B) "likewise" is a same direction conjunction, but notice the present tense verb "can." Dig a little deeper in sentence 11 and notice how Chuck Jones is described as *the **late** Chuck Jones*. That means he has passed away. We cannot use a present tense verb, as Chuck Jones is no longer capable of seeing because he is dead. Eliminate (B).

(C) "in addition to **this**…" what the heck is "this"? Let's not pick a sentence with an ambiguous pronoun. Eliminate (C).

Let's examine answer choices (D) and (E) together, as they both use the hypothetical tenses "could" and "would."

Perhaps the easiest difference to spot is the use of the "too" in (E), which acts as a transition from sentence 11 to sentence 12. The other answer choices clue me in to the fact that a transition is needed, so I would probably feel safest picking (E), but let's discuss the difference between "would" and "could."

Would's root word is "will," which indicates that if certain conditions were met (such as Jones still being alive) then definite things would happen (he would see similarities). *Could's* root word is "might" or "may," indicating that it is a possibility that something may happen. I think the writer is aiming for a definite, as he is writing a persuasive essay. The correct answer is (E).

Try an Improving Paragraphs section on your own with the following drill.

Improving Paragraphs Drill

(1) My brother has a special talent. (2) The skill to express himself perfectly through his artwork. (3) My brother is autistic, and has trouble expressing himself with words. (4) When he wants to convey something, he does so with paintings. (5) He concentrates intensely, lets his brushstrokes translate his thoughts, and my questions are seemingly answered by him with his finished work of art. (6) Even people who aren't related to him can understand what he is expressing. (7) Many people think that words are necessary for effective communication. (8) My brother, by all accounts, proves this point of view wrong, because he effectively communicates with friends, family, and strangers through his artwork every day.

(9) At school, my brother's teacher and friends benefit from his skill. (10) He does not fit within the required curriculum and organized lesson plan. (11) The teacher has been able to practice her flexibility, modifying lesson plans and curriculum to suit my brother's capabilities and talent. (12) Her abilities as a teacher are strengthened every day, as she learns and grows with my brother. (13) My brother's friends have learned to listen and communicate without words, which has strengthened their ability to express themselves. (14) Likewise, we choose the people we want to hang out with.

(15) My brother's talent affects his whole life. (16) His talent allows him to communicate with others so that he is part of the world, rather than living outside of it. (17) It allows him not to be a victim of his autism, but to make his diagnosis work for him. (18) Furthermore, it develops his artistic talent so that he can one day earn a living. (19) I am proud of my brother for both his talent and his ability to express himself through it.

30. Of the following, which is the best way to revise and combine sentences 1 and 2 (reproduced below)?

    My brother has a special talent. The skill to express himself perfectly through his artwork.

    (A) My brother has a special talent that includes the skill to express himself perfectly through his artwork.
    (B) Despite my brother's special talent, he still has the skill to express himself perfectly through his artwork.
    (C) My brother has a special talent and the skill to express himself perfectly through his artwork.
    (D) My brother has a special talent, it is the skill to express himself perfectly through his artwork.
    (E) My brother has a special talent: the skill to express himself perfectly through his artwork.

31. Of the following, which is the best way to phrase sentence 4 (reproduced below)?

    He concentrates intensely, lets his brushstrokes translate his thoughts, and my questions are seemingly answered by him with his finished work of art.

    (A) (As it is now)
    (B) As he concentrates intensely and lets his fingers translate his thoughts, he seems to be answering my questions with his finished work of art.
    (C) He concentrated intensely and let his fingers translate his thoughts, seeming to answer my questions with his finished work of art.
    (D) He concentrates intensely, lets his brushstrokes translate his thoughts, and then seems to answer all my questions with his finished work of art.
    (E) Concentrating intensely, he will let his brushstrokes translate his thoughts and then my questions are seemingly answered by him with his finished work of art.

32. In sentence 8, the phrase *by all accounts* is best replaced by

    (A) moreover
    (B) however
    (C) like my mother
    (D) to my knowledge
    (E) but nevertheless

33. Which of the following sentences should be omitted to improve the unity of the second paragraph?

    (A) Sentence 10
    (B) Sentence 11
    (C) Sentence 12
    (D) Sentence13
    (E) Sentence 14

34. In context, which of the following is the best way to phrase the underlined portion of sentence 18 (reproduced below)?

    Furthermore, it develops his artistic talent so that he can one day earn a living.

    (A) (As it is now)
    (B) Further developing
    (C) But it develops
    (D) However, he is developing
    (E) Considering this, he develops

35. A strategy that the writer uses within the third paragraph is to

    (A) digress from the main subject
    (B) use a defiant tone
    (C) repeat certain words and sentence patterns
    (D) make false assumptions and use hyperbole
    (E) use difficult vocabulary

Answers and Explanations

Answer Key:

30. (E)
31. (D)
32. (B)
33. (E)
34. (A)
35. (C)

30. Of the following, which is the best way to revise and combine sentences 1 and 2 (reproduced below)?

My brother has a special talent. The skill to express himself perfectly through his artwork.

(A) My brother has a special talent that includes the skill to express himself perfectly through his artwork.
(B) Despite my brother's special talent, he still has the skill to express himself perfectly through his artwork.
(C) My brother has a special talent and the skill to express himself perfectly through his artwork.
(D) My brother has a special talent, it is the skill to express himself perfectly through his artwork.
(E) My brother has a special talent: the skill to express himself perfectly through his artwork.

Sentence 2 is not a complete sentence and cannot, therefore, stand on its own. Let's see which one of the answer choices best links sentence 2 to sentence 1.

(A)   this answer is grammatically correct but seems to change the intended meaning of the sentence. His talent does not INCLUDE *the skill to express himself*, it *IS the skill to express himself*.

(B)   "despite" changes the direction of the sentence and indicates that his talent and his ability to express himself are *opposites*, rather than *the same thing*.

(C)   although the "and" is indeed a same direction word, it changes the meaning of the sentence, indicating that he *has a special talent* AND *the skill to express himself*. The talent and skill in this sentence are two separate things, rather than the same thing.

(D)   we have a run-on. Notice the visual: *("...talent, it...")*

(E)   the function of a colon is to set off a list or an explanation. *My brother has a special talent.* What is the talent? *The skill to express himself...* The colon links the two sentences together perfectly.

Correct Answer: (E)

122

31. Of the following, which is the best way to phrase sentence 4 (reproduced below)?

He concentrates intensely, lets his brushstrokes translate his thoughts, and my questions are seemingly answered by him with his finished work of art.

(A) (As it is now)
(B) As he concentrates intensely and lets his fingers translate his thoughts, he seems to be answering my questions with his finished work of art.
(C) He concentrated intensely and let his fingers translate his thoughts, seeming to answer my questions with his finished work of art.
(D) He concentrates intensely, lets his brushstrokes translate his thoughts, and then seems to answer all my questions with his finished work of art.
(E) Concentrating intensely, he will let his brushstrokes translate his thoughts and then my questions are seemingly answered by him with his finished work of art.

(A)   as written, this sentence is not **parallel** and is **passive**. "Concentrates" is a verb, "lets" is a verb, and "my questions" gives us a pronoun and noun. We need to have a verb to make the comma series parallel. *My questions are answered by him* is passive. *He answers my questions* would be active, which is always the better choice.

(B)   is definitely better than (A) but slightly changes the meaning of the sentence. The insertion of the "as" indicates that everything is *occurring simultaneously*. The questions are answered with the FINISHED piece of art, which indicates that things are not occurring simultaneously, but *chronologically*.

(C)   switches to the past tense. His brother is STILL making art, so it shouldn't be past, but present tense.

(D)   fixes the parallelism error. "concentrates" is a verb, "lets" is a verb, and "seems to answer" is a verb. *He is answering* so the sentence is active as well.

(E)   Uses passive construction: *my questions are answered by him*... It also switches to future tense "will let," which is incorrect.

Correct Answer: (D)

32. In sentence 8, the phrase *by all accounts* is best
replaced by

(A) moreover
(B) however
(C) like my mother
(D) to my knowledge
(E) but nevertheless

by all accounts is a transitional phrase, so we need to link sentence 8 to sentence 7.

(7) Many people think that words are necessary
for effective communication. (8) My brother, by
all accounts, proves this point of view wrong,
because he effectively communicates with friends,
family, and strangers through his artwork every day.

Sentence 8 flips the direction from sentence 7. So we can eliminate (A) and (C). Notice how (C) inserts "like my mother," which is completely off-topic. Let's check the other answer choices.

(B)   "however" flips the direction of the sentence.
(D)   "to my knowledge" doesn't provide the flip we need.
(E)   "but" and "nevertheless" together are redundant. If "nevertheless" were alone, it would be a contender.

Correct Answer: (B)

33. Which of the following sentences should be omitted
to improve the unity of the second paragraph?

(A) Sentence 10
(B) Sentence 11
(C) Sentence 12
(D) Sentence13
(E) Sentence 14

You may have caught the awkwardness of one of these sentences on the first read-thru of the essay, but in case you missed it, let's go through the sentences one by one. Keep in mind that the topic sentence of the second paragraph is essentially its main idea: *At school, my brother's teacher and friends benefit from his skill.*

(A)   *He does not fit within the required curriculum and organized lesson plan.* Does this sentence support the paragraph's main idea? Seems to.
(B)   *The teacher has been able to practice her flexibility, modifying lesson plans and curriculum to suit my brother's capabilities and talent.* This sentence expands on the previous sentence by letting us know the role the teacher plays.
(C)   *Her abilities as a teacher are strengthened every day as she learns and grows with my brother.* This sentence indicates how the teacher benefits from his brother's skill.

(D)   *My brother's friends have learned to listen and communicate without words, which has strengthened their ability to express themselves.* This sentence describes how his brother's friends have benefitted, which falls in line with the main idea of the paragraph.

(E)   *Likewise, we choose the people we want to hang out with.* This sentence has nothing to do with his brother's skill or how it benefits the teacher or the other students. Let's omit it!

Correct Answer: (E)

34. In context, which of the following is the best way to phrase the underlined portion of sentence 18 (reproduced below)?

<u>Furthermore, it develops</u> his artistic talent so that he can one day earn a living.

(A) (As it is now)
(B) Further developing
(C) But it develops
(D) However, he is developing
(E) Considering this, he develops

There is a "furthermore" which is a transition word, so let's connect it to sentence 17.

(17) It allows him not to be a victim of his autism, but to make his diagnosis work for him. (18) Furthermore, it develops his artistic talent so that he can one day earn a living.

The transition of "furthermore" seems okay, as sentence 18 is listing another benefit of his brother's talent. Let's check the other answer choices to make sure we aren't missing something.

(B)   "developing" is an awkward "ing" that creates a sentence fragment.
(C)   "but" flips the direction of the sentence. As the two sentences go in the same direction, we don't want a conjunction that flips.
(D)   "however" flips the direction.
(E)   inserts the ambiguous pronoun "this," and makes it a cause and effect relationship, which is not the intended meaning of the sentence.

Correct Answer: (A)

35. A strategy that the writer uses within the third paragraph is to

(A) digress from the main subject
(B) use a defiant tone
(C) repeat certain words and sentence
   patterns
(D) make false assumptions and use
   hyperbole
(E) use difficult vocabulary

This is a general question, so be sure to skim the third paragraph before looking at the answer choices. Summarize paragraph 3 in your own words first: *It talks about how his talent affects his whole life and future.*

(A)   "digress" means to stray from the topic. Does it *digress* from the main subject? No. The third paragraph *expands* on the topic of the essay: *his brother's talent.*

(B)   "defiant" means disobedient. Is the tone *disobedient*? Not at all!

(C)   does the author repeat words and phrases? Go back and look. The word "talent" is repeated throughout, as is the sentence pattern "it allows."

(D)   "hyperbole" means exaggeration, and nowhere in the third paragraph does the author exaggerate or make false assumptions.

(E)   any vocab words you stumbled over? Hopefully not!

Correct Answer: (C)

Chapter 7
The Essay

You have 25 minutes to read a prompt and an assignment, brainstorm ideas, and then write an essay that consists of a well-supported and reasoned point of view. That's quite a lot to accomplish in 25 minutes. So let's make sure you have all the tools necessary to use that 25 minutes wisely.

Remember: The Essay is always Section 1, so have your mind and pencils sharpened and ready to go.

Essay Essentials:
- You must use a #2 pencil (no pen).
- Use the two lined answer sheets provided.
- Brainstorm on your test booklet.
- Make sure you write on-topic. Otherwise you'll get a big fat zero.
- Don't plagiarize.

> *Note: I just saved you 2 minutes. When you open your test booklet, immediately go to the box in the middle of the page. No need to read ANY of the directions above it.*

The Box

Let's analyze a sample box:

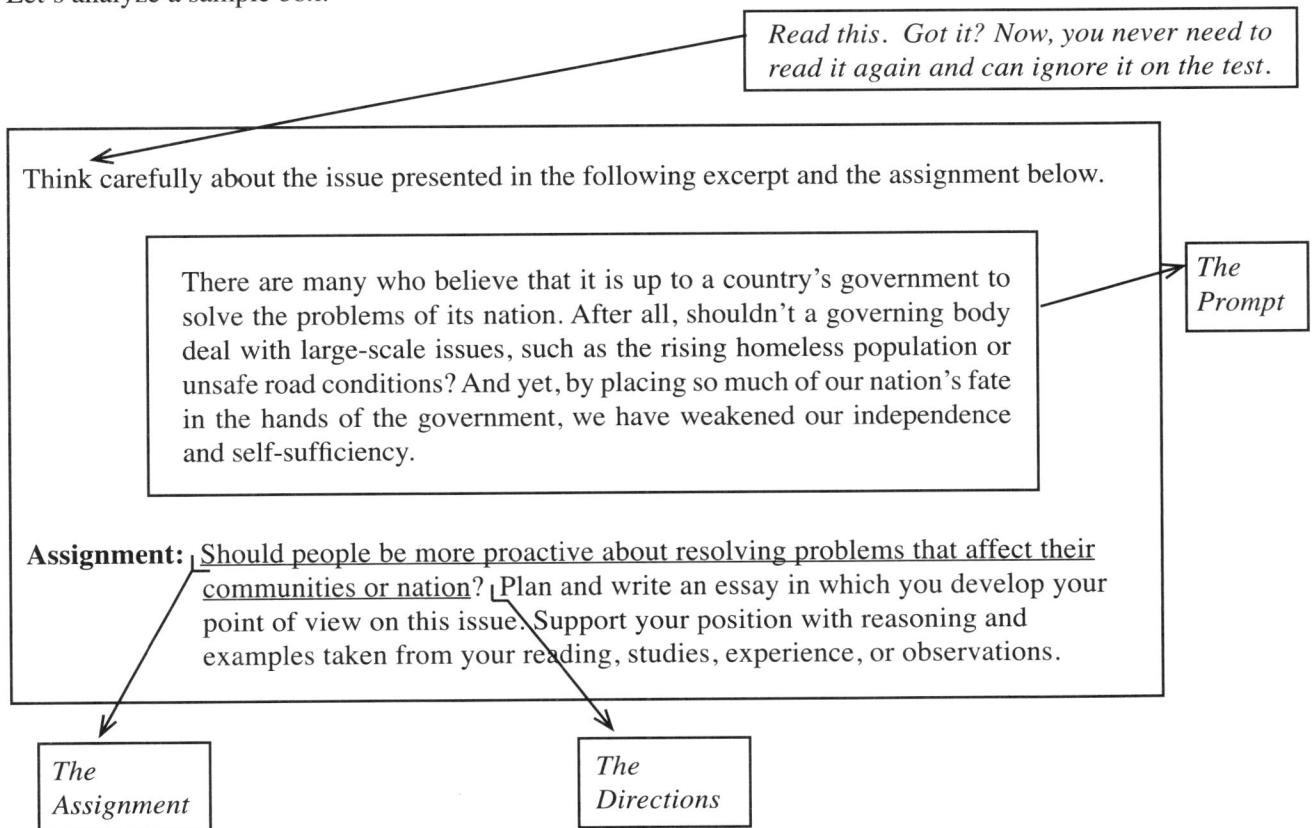

> *Read this. Got it? Now, you never need to read it again and can ignore it on the test.*

Think carefully about the issue presented in the following excerpt and the assignment below.

> There are many who believe that it is up to a country's government to solve the problems of its nation. After all, shouldn't a governing body deal with large-scale issues, such as the rising homeless population or unsafe road conditions? And yet, by placing so much of our nation's fate in the hands of the government, we have weakened our independence and self-sufficiency.

The Prompt

Assignment: Should people be more proactive about resolving problems that affect their communities or nation? Plan and write an essay in which you develop your point of view on this issue. Support your position with reasoning and examples taken from your reading, studies, experience, or observations.

The Assignment

The Directions

127

The Prompt: The box within the box always contains the prompt. You are NOT writing on the prompt. You do NOT need to refer to the prompt in your essay. You should NOT restate the prompt as your introductory sentence. You do NOT even have to read the prompt! It is simply there to kick-start your brain if need be. I confess: I NEVER read the prompt. I go straight to the assignment.

The Assignment: The first sentence of the assignment IS the assignment. THAT is the question you are answering and the ONLY sentence on the Section 1 essay page that you have to read. In this case: *Should people be more proactive about resolving problems that affect their communities or nation?*

The Directions: See all that junk after the question? Let's read and dissect it now so that you NEVER have to read it again. Don't worry; the directions never change.

*Plan and write an essay in which you **develop your point of view** on this issue. **Support your position** with reasoning and examples taken from your reading, studies, experience, or observations.*	Notice it says DEVELOP your point of view, not FIGURE IT OUT AS YOU GO. The mistake most students make is that they fill their essays with philosophy and abstraction, aka *fluff.* Tell us your point of view clearly and PROVE it to us with SPECIFIC examples. This means Literature, History, Current Events, and Personal Experiences.

What have we learned so far?

Open the test booklet, go straight to the assignment, read the question, and start brainstorming!

The Pacing

The following is a suggested pacing plan for writing your essays.

2 minutes - Read the Assignment and Brainstorm Examples

> *Note: Brainstorming your examples first helps you pick your thesis. Your thesis should be chosen based on your strongest examples.*

1 minute - Write your Thesis and Explanation of your Thesis
5-6 minutes - Write Intro Paragraph
12-13 minutes - Write Body Paragraphs
3-4 minutes - Write Conclusion

The Scoring

Your essay will be read and graded by two live readers: Teachers or college professors who have gone through a training program that makes them "expert" SAT graders. In other words, the system is flawed, because no matter what set of guidelines these graders are given, there is no black-and-white, right or wrong essay. The whole grading process is inherently subjective. This can work both for and against you.

ETS uses *holistic scoring* to grade your essays. Translation: Readers are told to score your essay based on the WHOLE, as opposed to penalizing you for every little thing you do wrong. They aren't supposed to dock points for minor grammatical errors, although if your essay contains glaring grammatical errors or a plethora of minor mistakes, you will be penalized. Readers are also told not to judge an essay by its length, but you can bet that the 4 or 5 paragraph essay is going to get a higher score than the 3 paragraph one.

Here's how it works: Two teachers give you a score on a scale of 1-6. 6 is the highest and 1 is the lowest. So if one reader gives you a 6 and the other gives you a 6, you have an essay score of 12, which is the best possible score. If one reader gives you a 6, and the other a 5, then you have an essay score of 11. If one reader were to give you a 5, and the other were to give you a 3, ETS calls in a third reader to determine which score is more on target.

You are shooting for a 10 or above. Here's why: *A 10 may help your grammar score, and it for sure won't hurt your grammar score.* A score of 9 or below will pull down a high multiple choice score (a score of 8 or 9 will only help a very low multiple choice score).

The Guidelines:

The essay scoring guide can be found in the *The Official SAT Study Guide* or online at the College Board website (www.collegeboard.org).

Let's break down the differences between a 6, 5, 4, and so on.

Score of 6

Develops a Point of View
- **Effectively** and **Insight-fully** with **Outstanding** Critical Thinking

Use of Examples
- **Clearly Appropriate**

Organization
- **Well** Organized/**Clearly** Focused

Language
- Used **Skillfully** with a **Varied** and **Accurate** Vocab

Sentence Structure
- **Meaningful Variety**

Grammar Errors
- **Free** of Most Errors

Score of 5

Develops a Point of View
- **Effectively** with **Strong** Critical Thinking

Use of Examples
- **Generally Appropriate**

Organization
- **Well** Organized/**Focused**

Language
- Used **Effectively** with **Appropriate** Vocab

Sentence Structure
- **Variety**

Grammar Errors
- **Generally Free** of Most Errors

Score of 4

Develops a Point of View
- With **Competent** Critical Thinking

Use of Examples
- **Adequate**

Organization
- **Generally** Organized/ Focused

Language
- Used **Adequately** but with **Inconsistently Appropriate** Vocab

Sentence Structure
- **Some** Variety

Grammar Errors
- **Some** Errors

Score of 3

Develops a Point of View
- With **Some** Critical Thinking

Use of Examples
- May use **Inadequate** examples

Organization
- **Limited** Organization/Focus

Language
- Used **Almost Adequately** but with **Occasionally Weak or Inappropriate** Vocab

Sentence Structure
- **Lacks** Variety

Grammar Errors
- **Accumulation of** Errors

Score of 2

Develops a Point of View
- **Vaguely** with **Weak** Critical Thinking

Use of Examples
- **Inappropriate** or **Insufficient**

Organization
- **Poor** Organization/Focus

Language
- Used **Adequately** with **Limited or Incorrect** Vocab

Sentence Structure
- **Frequent Problems**

Grammar Errors
- **Serious** Errors

Score of 1

Develops a Point of View
- **Doesn't** develop

Use of Examples
- **Very little** or **None**

Organization
- **Disorganized/Unfocused**

Language
- Displays **Fundamental Errors**

Sentence Structure
- **Severely Flawed**

Grammar Errors
- **Serious** and **Pervasive** Errors

The Look

The readers aren't supposed to grade your essay based on your handwriting or the essay's length, but the look of your essay does count, as the scores just can't help but be subjective in nature.

If a student hands me an essay I can't read because her handwriting is sloppy, and I have to struggle to decipher the first paragraph, I don't even finish reading the essay; I just give it a score of 2. Keep in mind: if your SAT tutor doesn't have the patience to figure out your scribble, the reader certainly doesn't have the time or the desire to learn your cryptic handwriting. They have 2 minutes to spend on your essay. How about you help yourself out by writing a legible essay that is easy for them to read? They will appreciate it, and your score will reflect that appreciation.

Sloppy handwriting is not the same as an actual handwriting disability. If you have been diagnosed with **Dysgraphia** go to the College Board website and find the *Services for Students with Disabilities* page to see about getting accommodations, such as permission to write your essay using a computer.

Get the Look:

- Bring four sharpened #2 pencils. When a pencil starts to get dull, switch it out with a sharpened one.
- Create, shape, and write a 4-5 paragraph essay.
- Indent paragraphs using the length of your thumb.
- Don't cross out. ERASE. That's why pencils have erasers.
- Fill up the two pages as best you can. LENGTH LOOKS GOOD.
- If you need to add a thought use a caret (^) and write above.
- Write as NEATLY as you possibly can.

Where to write? Use the two lined sheets ETS includes in your test booklet. We've included sample sheets for you at the end of this chapter. You only get two sheets so use your space wisely!

That's the surface of your essay; now let's talk about the substance!

Essay Structure

Your essay should be at least 4 paragraphs: An *Introductory Paragraph*, *2 Body Paragraphs*, and a *Conclusion Paragraph*.

Introductory Paragraph

- The very first element your intro paragraph needs is a ***Hook*** – a sentence (or two or three) at the beginning of your essay that entices the reader to keep reading. Your hook needs to capture the reader's attention. Make an entrance!

Different types of Hooks:

The Quote ————————————————————————————→ Memorize 3 to 5 quotes that grab you. You can always use one of these as your hook. Quotes are a great way to get the essay moving!

"A lie gets halfway around the world before the truth has a chance to get its pants on." Sir Winston Churchill aptly captured the damaging nature of a lie, whether that lie be a tasty bit of gossip, or a falsehood that influences on a global scale.

Don't forget: you need a sentence that ties the quote back to the rest of your essay!

The Shocking Declaration ————————————————————→ It's a good tactic to be clear in your point of view and add a bit of surprise to hook the reader, even if your p.o.v. is a tad extreme.

Every human being has within them the capacity for unimaginable evil. It is only because of the balance and order of societal constraints that this malevolence is suppressed.

The Hypothetical Scenario ————————————————————→ This is a great type of hook to use, especially if you're stuck on a lead-in.

Imagine gaining all the success you've strived for, only to look around and realize you are totally alone. You have burned all your bridges and have no true friends, but you are basking in money and fame.

The Rhetorical Question ————————————————————→ This is my least favorite of the hooks, but perfectly acceptable. Try to limit your rhetorical questions to 3.

How would you feel if you were unable to ask the question: Why? How would you cope if you were unable to challenge the assumptions of your peers, supervisors, or loved ones? If you were forced to accept their absolute power with no chance of expressing your own voice and needs?

The Anecdote ————————————————→ This is one of my favorite types of hooks. Start looking around and gathering your anecdotes. Life is full of them!

I was driving my four-year-old nephew to Little League practice, and in front of us was a truck full of tires. My nephew clapped his hands together and squealed, "Look! It's a playground!" That childlike ability to see the world rose-colored and paint the blandest of images with imagination is a skill to protect no matter how old we grow.

The Statistic ————————————————→ Show how smart you are by coming in with specific knowledge at the very beginning of your essay.

Half of all American children come from divorced homes and approximately half of these kids will witness the disintegration of a parent's second marriage as well.

The Analogy ————————————————→ A great type of hook for you creative types out there.

Watching my grandparents together is like watching a beautiful dance. They know each other's rhythms, they move at the same count, and they can tell what the other needs by a flick of the wrist or a slight movement in step.

> *Note: The hook can be a single sentence or several. No matter the length, it leads you to your thesis.*

- The second element your intro paragraph needs is a *Thesis* – your argument or point of view.

In order to test your thesis, ask: *Do I clearly answer the question?*

- The third element is an *Explanation of the Thesis* - it is not enough to merely answer the question, you must expand on your thesis and explain WHY you think the way you do.

In order to test your explanation, ask: *Do I explain why I have the opinion I do?*

> *Note: You do not ever need to use the words "I think..." or "I believe..." You are the author of the essay, so we know it is you who is doing the thinking and the believing. That being said, you can use the pronoun "I" throughout your essay. How else are you to provide personal observations?*

Examples of Thesis with Explanation:

Question: *Is the majority always right?*

- The majority is always right because as human beings we have inherent instincts that manifest themselves in the actions and thoughts of the majority. → Explanation of Thesis

→ Thesis

Question: *Do changes that make our lives easier, make them better?*

- Ease does not equal superiority. Changes, such as advancements in technology or an influx of unexpected wealth, might make our lives easier, but they do not necessarily make our lives better. With ease comes a certain idleness, and some changes can eliminate opportunities to grow and mature that hard work and suffering might otherwise inspire.

→ Explanation of Thesis/This could also arguably be a Hook!

→ Look how the student has introduced his examples. This is great!

→ Thesis

→ Explanation of Thesis

Question: *Should people who say what they think when others lack the courage to speak their minds be considered heroes?*

- Every morning my alarm clock wakes me up to a Rush Limbaugh diatribe. It is the only sound that gets me right out of bed, as I can't wait to hush him up. I need to give the man credit for speaking his mind and exercising the right to freedom of speech that America protects, but I would not say that he is a hero simply because he espouses conservative politics on a nationally syndicated radio show. Speaking one's mind when others lack the courage to do so, while brave in some respects, does not earn one the title of hero. Many people say what they think at the expense of other's feelings and speak out of selfishness and ignorance. A better example of a hero would be a person who sacrifices his/her personal agenda for the good of humanity as a whole, continually engaging in brave and noble deeds and words.

→ Hook. What type? The Anecdote.

→ Thesis

→ Explanation of Thesis. This student has totally explained WHY.

- The fourth and final element of our intro is a *List of Examples* – let the reader know what you are going to be detailing in your essay. It is a road map the reader will appreciate.

Samples of List of Examples:

The detainment of Japanese Americans in internment camps in WWII and the hate crimes committed against Muslims in America, are examples that illustrate the violence and misunderstanding that can be caused by ignorance and insularity.

→ List of Examples

→ Connection to Thesis

The naïve idea that conscience is a stronger motivator than fame, money, or power disintegrates when one considers Hitler's horrific crimes during WWII, and more recently Bernard Madoff's billion-dollar scandal on Wall Street.

→ Connection to Thesis

→ List of Examples

Let's put an entire Introductory Paragraph together:

Question: *Do people spend too much time trying to satisfy others, rather than just trying to satisfy their own standards?*

- "I swear, by my life and my love of it, that I will never live for the sake of another man, nor ask another man to live for mine." With these words, Russian-born American novelist and philosopher Ayn Rand sums up her philosophy of Objectivism: that man's highest moral purpose is to live for his own rational needs and interests, never sacrificing himself for others, or expecting others to sacrifice for him. If people first satisfied their own standards, they would have more to give to society, and in nurturing their own desires, needs, and gifts, would inherently be satisfying others. People do indeed spend too much time satisfying others; time that would be better spent satisfying their own standards. A dissection of the events in Shel Silverstein's The Giving Tree and an analysis of the success of laissez-faire capitalism, confirm that satisfying your own desires should be the utmost priority.

→ Hook. What type? The Quote. Notice how she attributes the quote to the correct person (Rand) and uses it to usher in an explanation of her thesis.

→ Explanation of Thesis

→ Thesis – we pretty much already know her thesis before she states it here, but notice how she doesn't leave anything for the reader to assume, but instead CLEARLY states her thesis.

List of Examples – notice how she connects them to her thesis.

Body Paragraphs

The first thing your body paragraphs need is a ***transition***. Either a transition from the introductory paragraph, or a transition from the 1st body paragraph. Transitions are connections from one idea to the next or from one paragraph to the next. Think of transitions as bridges.

Examples of Transitions:

Transitions from Intro paragraph to 1st Body Paragraph:

- The mass protests in January 2011 against Egyptian President Mubarak illustrate just how powerful the will of a people against authoritarian rule can be.

→ Introduction of body paragraph example.

→ Connects the example to the thesis and the intro paragraph.

- Technological advancements come with a price, as witnessed by the rising rate of obesity in American children.

→ Reiteration of thesis ties in to the example.

136

Transition from 1st body paragraph to 2nd body paragraph:

- We look not only to flesh and blood characters to inspire a positive outlook, but also to familiar story book characters, such as Cinderella, to motivate a fresh perspective.

Here, the author acknowledges the previous example (I would imagine an example of someone from history) and relates it back to her thesis.

Transitions to her second example, Cinderella, and again relates it back to her thesis.

- The second element of your body paragraphs should be ***detailing your example***. This is perhaps the trickiest part. Either students don't go into enough detail, or they go into too much detail.

Tips:

Assume the reader knows nothing of your example. If you are writing about Huck Finn, do not assume the reader has read the book. The reader has no idea who Huck or Jim is, so you had better let him/her know. You should start with a simple synopsis of plot, and an introduction of the characters your example refers to. Follow with specific details from the novel that help to prove your thesis. It is not enough to say that Huck escapes the racist viewpoints of his neighbors through his friendship with Jim; you must SHOW a specific example of their friendship that causes Huck to deny the racist impulses of the South.

If you are using Martin Luther King, Jr. as your example, do not assume the reader has any idea who Martin Luther King, Jr. is. While you do not need to tell us King's whole life story, you do need to tell us that he was a civil rights leader. You should not merely say that he greatly influenced the civil rights movement; you have to show us specifically HOW he did so. Check out the difference:

- Martin Luther King, Jr. was a famous speaker who influenced the civil rights movement and helped end segregation.

Vs.

- Through non-violent protests, boycotts, and marches on Washington, D.C., Martin Luther King, Jr. used his oratory skills and fervent belief in equality to lead the civil rights movement in America, helping to end segregation and battle discrimination against minorities.

Do you see how much more specific and effective the second option is?

- Finally, your body paragraphs must have a **_Thesis Connection_** – how does your example relate back to your thesis and PROVE your point? Don't expect the reader to put the connection together, you have to hold the reader by the hand and tell her specifically HOW it relates back to your thesis.

Don't forget that the reader does not have telepathic powers and can't get inside your brain to figure out what you were thinking. That is why clarity of thought is incredibly important. Leave no room for the reader to guess, assume, or fill in all the open holes in your essay. Because they won't. They will just deduct points.

Example of Thesis Connection:

Question: *Is knowledge a benefit, or a burden?*

- Knowledge can most certainly be a burden when it tests your sense of right and wrong and loyalty to a friend. My best friend confessed to me that she was only passing chemistry class because she was getting the answers to the tests from a fellow student. She swore me to secrecy and then smiled with relief. "So good to get that off my chest and tell someone," she said. However, I was now left with the burden of that secret. I wanted to unload that knowledge onto someone else, and my strong sense of right and wrong compelled me to inform our chemistry teacher. My equally strong sense of loyalty to my best friend held me back. As a compromise, I confronted my best friend. "I will help you study and pass the chemistry tests, but you have to promise to stop cheating," I said. She accepted the deal and we studied hard for the rest of the semester, but I will never forget the strain her secret put on me, making me wary of the knowledge others willingly pass on.

Transition from thesis to specific example.

Thesis Connection

Thesis Connection

Detail of example – not too much, and not too little. Certainly no superfluous information here.

Thesis Connection – she connects her example to her thesis (knowledge can be a burden) throughout her body paragraph.

Let's put an entire Body Paragraph together:

Question: *Are we born with our identity, or is identity something we create ourselves?*

- Another example in which true identity is shown through one's actions is in the novel, <u>Percy Jackson & the Olympians: The Lightning Thief.</u> The protagonist, Percy, is the son of a human and the Greek god Poseidon. It is revealed early on that the lightning bolts of Zeus, the supreme ruler of the gods, have been stolen, and Zeus blames Poseidon's son Percy, thinking that Poseidon is trying to usurp his place as king of the gods. Percy, however, embarks on a quest to retrieve the bolts from the real enemy of the gods, Luke. Percy succeeds and returns the bolts to Zeus, who changes his view of Percy. Through his heroic actions, Percy reveals that his true identity is not the one given to him at birth, but the one he created himself.

We have a basic Transition but it is really all you need. Notice how he reiterates his thesis (we create identity through our actions).

Remember to always underline book titles. I would like it better if he had included the author: *Another example in which true identity is shown through one's actions is in Rick Riordan's novel, <u>Percy Jackson & the Olympians: The Lightning Thief</u>.*

Fabulous level of detail. He goes into just enough background information and only shares details from the book that support his thesis.

Thesis Connection

Conclusion

There are three components to your Conclusion: ***Restate your Thesis***, ***Relist your Examples***, and add a ***Final Thought***. The ***Final Thought*** shows that you understand the problem at hand in a greater context than simply the scenario being addressed.

It is imperative that your essay has a conclusion. If you are running out of time and need to sacrifice the thoroughness of your 2nd or 3rd body paragraph, then do so for the sake of the conclusion. If you only have time for a one-sentence conclusion, then so be it. ***A one-sentence conclusion is better than no conclusion***.

Examples of Conclusions:

Question: *Do we need adversity in order to truly understand ourselves?*

- Adversity strengthens our resolve and highlights aspects of our personality that we may wish to foster, or squelch. As witnessed by the fortitude of survivors such as Christopher Reeve and Helen Keller, adversity can manifest amazing bravery in those who have the courage to embrace it. May we likewise look adversity squarely in the eyes and welcome it the next time it comes calling.

Restatement of Thesis

Relist of Examples – even better, she connected it to her thesis.

Final Thought

Question: *Is it sometimes better to take a risk, than to follow a safe course of action?*

- If it were not for such courageous pioneers as the Wright Brothers and Neil Armstrong, humans might still be land bound. These aviators did not follow the safe path, but let their imaginations soar and took the ultimate risk. Without the capacity to challenge fear and take a risk, human beings would not be nearly as high on the evolutionary ladder.

→ Relist of Examples

→ Restate Thesis

→ Final Thought

Note: Order doesn't matter. You can start with a Final Thought and end with your Thesis or vice versa. Just try to have all the elements somewhere in your conclusion!

Here is the Essay Formula in skeletal form:

Introduction:
- *Hook*
- *Thesis*
- *Explanation of Thesis*
- *List of Examples*

Body Paragraphs:
- *Transition*
- *Detail your Example*
- *Thesis Connection*

Conclusion:
- *Restate Thesis*
- *Relist Examples*
- *Final Thought*

To Agree or Not to Agree

⟶ **To agree or to disagree**

One is not better than the other, as long as you pick a side and prove it. Don't waver. If you agree, agree wholeheartedly. If you disagree, fight for your opinion.

Typically, we will read the question and our mind immediately answers, "Ah, yes, I agree," or "Oh no, that's the stupidest thing I've ever heard." Don't let your mind dictate your answer to the question, let your examples. Brainstorm your examples first. If your strongest examples support the argument, then agree. Disagree if your best examples don't support the argument.

> *Note: Sometimes, it is helpful to disagree with a statement that you actually agree with. This approach seems counterintuitive, but often leads to clearer, more persuasive and well-supported essays. Reason being, not only are you trying to convince other people of your opinion, but you are also trying to convince yourself. Students end up with fewer holes in their essays, because they haven't made any assumptions. Disagreeing with yourself slows your brain down so that you move from point to point more carefully.*

⟶ **Acknowledging the counter argument**

Sure, you can give a nod to the counter argument, but briefly and succinctly. Spend your time proving yourself right, not focusing on what the opposing side will use against you.

Examples

Students normally don't freak out about finding a point of view, they freak out about finding examples to support that point of view. The biggest fear I hear is, *What if I can't think of anything?* The most common justification for a low essay score: *I spent 10 minutes just sitting there trying to think of an example!* A legitimate fear, and an even more legitimate excuse, until I tell you that the trick is to have your examples prepared beforehand. It is your job to come up with 3 history examples, 3 current events, 3 literature examples, and 3 personal experiences. Add some anecdotes and perhaps some examples from pop culture, art, or music to the mix and you have about 15 examples from which to choose. Trust me, 2 of those examples will be applicable to whatever essay question ETS asks. That cuts 10 minutes of brainstorming down to 2.

When I say, come up with your examples beforehand, I mean know these examples inside out. Research them, know the key players involved, think about what theses you could apply these examples to. For instance, the global response to the tsunami in Japan can be used to support the idea that people have a responsibility for not only their communities but also for the world at large. It could support an essay debating man vs. nature; it could even support the claim that adversity is necessary and in the long run beneficial.

When researching your examples from literature use Spark Notes or CliffsNotes. Read all the CliffsNotes; reacquaint yourself with the characters, the plot, the themes. Memorize the information you have gathered.

Once you have collected your examples, pick several essay questions from the *Official Guide* or the College Board website and write a paragraph for each of these examples. Practice leads to perfection! Or at least a score of 10.

Good Examples vs. Bad Examples

Here are the examples most students use:

Martin Luther King, Jr.
Hitler
Gandhi
Rosa Parks
Huck Finn
The Great Gatsby
The Scarlett Letter

These topics are certainly not off limits, but it might behoove you to get a bit more creative with your examples.

Note: Don't be too broad with your examples. WWII should not be used as an example. Italy's role in WWII would be a better example because it is more specific and narrow. Don't talk about the American Revolution; rather talk about a specific battle in the American Revolution.

Common Grammatical Errors

The errors that occur most frequently on the essay are **pronoun errors**, **sentence fragments**, and **run-ons**.

To avoid grammar mistakes, edit your essay as you go. Don't get so hung up that you don't push forward and finish in the allotted time, but reread each paragraph before moving on to the next. Our hands can't keep up with our speedy heads, so slow down and give your hands a chance to catch up.

Pronoun Errors: Pronoun Ambiguity is the most common mistake I see. Be cautious of using the infamous *this, that,* or *it.* Make sure the reader can identify what "it" is, or who "he" is. It is better to be repetitive than ambiguous.

Examples of Pronoun Ambiguity/Agreement:

Percy succeeds in returning the bolts to Zeus and his view changes. → Whose view? *Percy's view* or *Zeus's view?*

Many people would rather be honest than tell lies. However, it is not always bad, because people can lie with good intentions. → The "it" is not clear. Try this instead: *"However, telling lies is not always bad…"*

Technological advancements are not always beneficial. These come with a price, as witnessed by the rising rate of obesity in American children. → What the heck is "these?" Clarify – *"Technological progress comes with a price…"*

142

Pronoun Agreement errors show up almost as much as ambiguity. Check out a classic Pronoun Agreement mistake:

It is important to challenge the authority of the government, as they ⟶ *don't always have the needs of the minority in mind.*

Who is "they?" I think it is pretty clear *they* refers to *government*, but "government" is singular and "they" is plural, so the *they* should be *it*!

Sentence Fragments/Run-ons: Students rushing and not editing as they go cause the majority of these errors. You must re-read to catch fragments and run-ons!

Jonathan was not calling the sixth grader names, he *explained how he was simply telling the truth and did not mean to harm her.*

Here is your run-on error. Two independent clauses cannot be separated by only a comma!

By always telling the truth can make friends turn away from you.

Careful of those awkward "ings!" They create fragments! It's an easy fix: Just remove the "by."

Let's put everything we've learned together, and analyze a couple of SAT essays.

Question: *Do we need other people in order to understand ourselves?*

Essay #1

      Philosophers have wondered for centuries what man is capable of, both individually and on a societal level. In ancient times, Greeks put humans to the test in the Olympic games, attempting to determine their capabilities by pushing them to physical extremes. However, the people of that time were actually in search of the answer to a larger question; they were looking to understand one's inner being. But looking inside one's true nature requires a mirror, and what better mirror than the larger consciousness of one's entire community. History presents numerous examples that demonstrate that to truly understand oneself, one must look to the motivations and accomplishments of society as a whole.

      The Civil War is a historical event that clearly illustrates the capabilities and drive of Americans. In 1860, when Abraham Lincoln won the presidential election, numerous southern states seceded from the Union, which ultimately led the country into war in an effort to reunite America. In more recent times of peril, the United States has not hesitated to go to war, illustrating that Americans are capable of fighting and putting their lives on the line for what they believe. On September 11, 2001, when America was struck by terrorists in New York City, she rose to the occasion to battle terrorism. This war still wages on in 2006 and is an ever-present reminder of American's capacity to fight for their beliefs. The strength and success in these dramatic events are obvious portrayals of Americans, a people with strong beliefs and the will to accomplish their goals.

      Although America has excelled as a superpower, the sense of community inspired by our forefathers continues to shape the reactions of our people. Take for instance, the devastating strike of Hurricane Katrina, which occurred in August, 2005. Just last year, a class five storm struck the American South and caused a state of emergency throughout the area. Hundreds were killed and the destruction was widespread. In response, America took action, both in the political and private arenas. Americans from all over the country chipped in volunteer efforts and financial aid to those in need, clearly depicting America as a whole, a group of individuals with strong moral convictions and an enthusiasm to support those in need. By looking at the actions of our community, we have a clear glimpse into ourselves.

History is a natural place to explore in order to discover what human nature encompasses. Events such as the Civil War and Hurricane Katrina represent what Americans are capable of and from these situations it can be understood who Americans, both collectively and individually, truly are. Though the Greeks may have been on the right track with the Olympic games, the prowess they witnessed was merely physical. To dig deeper and to understand oneself, one must look to a much more substantial event to see what he and his fellow humans are truly capable of.

Let's review the strengths and weaknesses of each paragraph before moving on to our second essay.

Philosophers have wondered for centuries what man is capable of, both individually and on a societal level. In ancient times, Greeks put humans to the test in the Olympic games, attempting to determine their capabilities by pushing them to physical extremes. However, the people of that time were actually in search of the answer to a larger question; they were looking to understand one's inner being. But looking inside one's true nature requires a mirror, and what better mirror than the larger consciousness of one's entire community. History presents numerous examples that demonstrate that to truly understand oneself, one must look to the motivations and accomplishments of society as a whole.

HOOK –The hook is an example in and of itself.

EXPLANATION of THESIS – notice how this student wrote his explanation BEFORE he laid out his thesis.

LIST of EXAMPLES – keeping it general with "history" is not my favorite way to list examples. It would have been better to write: *"Americans' readiness to fight for democracy and ability to recover from catastrophic events such as Hurricane Katrina demonstrate that…"*

THESIS – notice how this student got a bit more sophisticated and didn't just say, "yes, we need others to understand ourselves." He made the topic his own by getting specific, *"we need to look to the accomplishments of society as a whole to understand who we are individually."*

The Civil War is a historical event that clearly illustrates the capabilities and drive of Americans. In 1860, when Abraham Lincoln won the presidential election, numerous southern states seceded from the Union, which ultimately led the country into war in an effort to reunite America. In more recent times of peril, the United States has not hesitated to go to war, illustrating that Americans are capable of fighting and putting their lives on the line for what they believe. On September 11, 2001, when America was struck by terrorists in New York City, she rose to the occasion to battle terrorism. This war still wages on in 2006 and is an ever-present reminder of American's capacity to fight for their beliefs. The strength and success in these dramatic events are obvious portrayals of Americans, a people with strong beliefs and the will to accomplish their goals.

Although America has excelled as a superpower, the sense of community inspired by our forefathers continues to shape the reactions of our people. Take for instance, the devastating strike of Hurricane Katrina, which occurred in August, 2005. Just last year, a class five storm struck the American South and caused a state of emergency through-out the area. Hundreds were killed and the destruction was widespread. In response, America took action, both in the political and private arenas. Americans from all over the country chipped in volunteer efforts and financial aid to those in need, clearly depicting America as a whole, a group of individuals with strong moral convictions and an enthusiasm to support those in need. By looking at the actions of our community, we have a clear glimpse into ourselves.

History is a natural place to explore in order to discover what human nature encompasses. Events such as the Civil War and Hurricane Katrina represent what Americans are capable of and from these situations it can be understood who Americans, both collectively and individually, truly are. Though the Greeks may have been on the right track with the Olympic games, the prowess they witnessed was merely physical. To dig deeper and to understand oneself, one must look to a much more substantial event to see what he and his fellow humans are truly capable of.

TRANSITION – well, sort of. We have a transition from HISTORY in the intro to a HISTORICAL EVENT in body paragraph 1, but we jump to AMERICANS and don't really tie this jump in to our thesis. There is a chance the reader might get lost. Had he used my option for listing examples – *"Americans' readiness to fight for democracy and ability to recover from catastrophic events such as Hurricane Katrina demonstrate that…"* the transition to the first body paragraph would have been much clearer.

LEVEL of DETAIL - Would have been better with an additional sentence to amp up the detail, such as: *"Police and rescue workers from all over the nation traveled to NYC to help in the recovery efforts, and blood donations across the nation increased."*

He hasn't provided a THESIS CONNECTION. Ideally he would want a connection, such as: *"Looking to society as a whole and understanding what it means to be an American, helps me better understand my true nature."* Yes – you can use "I" in the essay and make it personal!

TRANSITION – perfect!

LEVEL of DETAIL – appropriate level of detail.

RESTATEMENT of THESIS – great! He connected this example to his thesis.

RELIST EXAMPLES – great! And he tied these examples into his thesis.

RESTATE THESIS – great!

Introduction

While I appreciate the sophistication of the hook and thesis, don't feel like you can't keep it simple. Such cleverness is not expected or necessary. What I love is that he didn't fill the intro paragraph with a bunch of abstract fluff and philosophy. Everything he wrote supported his thesis and he wasn't repetitive with his thoughts (meaning he didn't say the same thing three times in different ways). Save the repetition for a restatement of your thesis in your body paragraphs! And he didn't use the intro to figure out what his thesis was going to be.

⟶ **The reader can tell when you're floating along trying to FIND what to say, rather than KNOWING what you want to say.**

It is clear he knew his thesis BEFORE he set pen to paper. Notice how pretty much every part of the intro is highlighted. That means it is filled with ONLY the essentials, as it should be. Bravo!

Body Paragraph #1

The transition is so-so, and the level of detail is adequate. He tells me the date of the Civil War, he knows who the president was, and he tells me the reason the Civil War occurred. He doesn't tell me how this example proves his thesis, but that's okay, because he gives a related example and ties them together at the end. He transitions to his second example (Sept. 11th) quite nicely, and goes into a sufficient level of detail. A sentence detailing just how Americans rose to the occasion might have been a nice addition. I do think his thesis connection is weak. He explains how these two events help portray the character of *Americans*, but does he connect this to his more general thesis: to truly understand *oneself*? He should have indicated how looking at these events and ascertaining the characteristics of America help him understand his motivations on an individual level.

Body Paragraph #2

The transition is great, and I love the level of detail. He expands on the concept of looking at America as a whole and connects it to his thesis with the final sentence. This is what you are going for with those body paragraphs.

⟶ **He is PROVING his point to me.**

Conclusion

What I love is that he rounds out his essay by bringing it back to the Olympic example, which was his hook. Not necessary, but a nice trick. He relists his examples and restates his thesis. An altogether great conclusion!

As a whole, I think this is a great essay. He lost me for a bit in the second paragraph, but he got right back on track in the third. It was easy to read, which makes the reader's job more pleasant. This essay would get a solid score somewhere in the 10-12 range.

Let's look at another essay that answers the same question - *do we need other people in order to understand ourselves* - but in an entirely different way. Analyze the essay on your own first, before you look at my analysis.

Essay #2

There exist people who possess the unnerving gift of self-reflection: the Dr. Phils who preach the psychologically healthy frame of mind and the Mother Theresas so pure of heart self-reflection is second nature. But the majority of us humans are so consumed by ego that our view of ourselves is blurred, the edges soft and the truth obscured. We need other people to occasionally hold up a mirror and say, "this is who you really are." Such reflectors are found in the persons of Gandhi, as well as the many individuals who cross our paths.

For years, India existed as a submissive British colony, her resources and culture diluted by the Mother Country. It took a single man, Gandhi, to take a stand, hold up a mirror to his fellow countrymen and remind them that they are Indians, and that India belonged to them. Thru nonviolent resistance in the form of peaceful protest and hunger strikes, Gandhi helped his people discover their true nature, sparking a resistance that eventually earned India her freedom.

Each day I see a glimpse of myself in my interactions with others. Just this morning, with a veritable downpour to accompany me, I was walking from 7-Eleven to my car, when a man carrying a bike and wearing an orange vest stopped me. "Excuse me," he began, "I work at the VA and my tire is flat. I need a pump to get home. I live all the way downtown and it's cold and raining." I hesitated, not wanting to be taken advantage of. "How much is a pump?" I asked. "Five bucks," he responded. Just the amount of cash in my wallet. I tossed over the money. "God bless you," he smiled a toothy grin. "You saved me. You're a good person." Hearing those words reflected so sincerely made me smile in turn. But I didn't let myself off the hook that easily. I had to acknowledge that my first reaction was one of resistance. While we need others to better understand ourselves, we must still be equipped with the ability to self-reflect.

The ego is a powerful motivator and difficult to manage on our own. We need other awesome individuals like Gandhi, or a simple man in an orange vest, to tame our egos and let our true lights shine.

Now let's analyze this second essay, checking to see if it has all the necessary components.

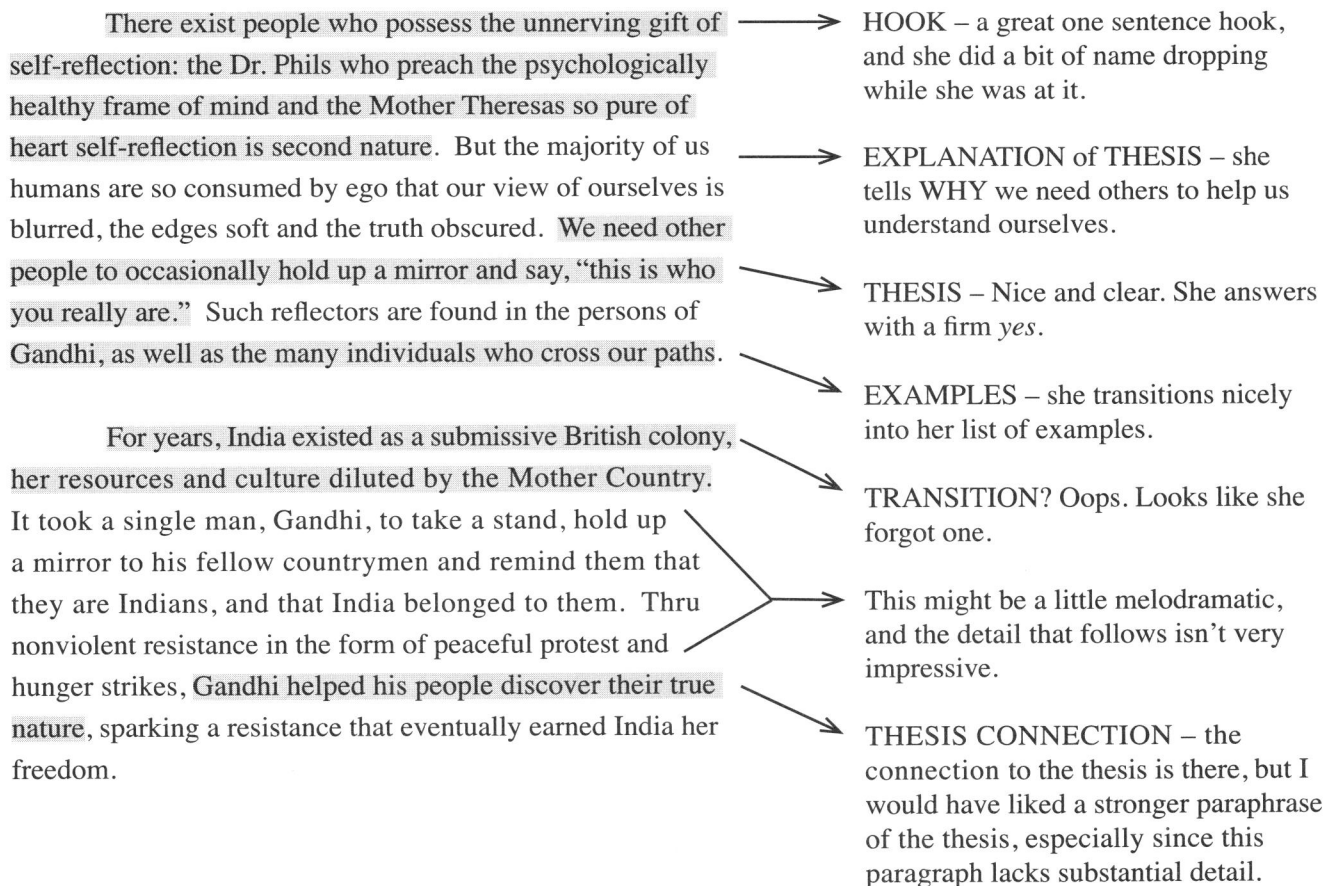

There exist people who possess the unnerving gift of self-reflection: the Dr. Phils who preach the psychologically healthy frame of mind and the Mother Theresas so pure of heart self-reflection is second nature. But the majority of us humans are so consumed by ego that our view of ourselves is blurred, the edges soft and the truth obscured. We need other people to occasionally hold up a mirror and say, "this is who you really are." Such reflectors are found in the persons of Gandhi, as well as the many individuals who cross our paths.

HOOK – a great one sentence hook, and she did a bit of name dropping while she was at it.

EXPLANATION of THESIS – she tells WHY we need others to help us understand ourselves.

THESIS – Nice and clear. She answers with a firm *yes*.

EXAMPLES – she transitions nicely into her list of examples.

For years, India existed as a submissive British colony, her resources and culture diluted by the Mother Country. It took a single man, Gandhi, to take a stand, hold up a mirror to his fellow countrymen and remind them that they are Indians, and that India belonged to them. Thru nonviolent resistance in the form of peaceful protest and hunger strikes, Gandhi helped his people discover their true nature, sparking a resistance that eventually earned India her freedom.

TRANSITION? Oops. Looks like she forgot one.

This might be a little melodramatic, and the detail that follows isn't very impressive.

THESIS CONNECTION – the connection to the thesis is there, but I would have liked a stronger paraphrase of the thesis, especially since this paragraph lacks substantial detail.

Each day I see a glimpse of myself in my interactions with others. Just this morning, with a veritable downpour to accompany me, I was walking from 7-Eleven to my car, when a man carrying a bike and wearing an orange vest stopped me. "Excuse me," he began, "I work at the VA and my tire is flat. I need a pump to get home. I live all the way downtown and it's cold and raining." I hesitated, not wanting to be taken advantage of. "How much is a pump?" I asked. "Five bucks," he responded. Just the amount of cash in my wallet. I tossed over the money. "God bless you," he smiled a toothy grin. "You saved me. You're a good person." Hearing those words reflected so sincerely made me smile in turn. But I didn't let myself off the hook that easily. I had to acknowledge that my first reaction was one of resistance. While we need others to better understand ourselves, we must still be equipped with the ability to self-reflect.

The ego is a powerful motivator and difficult to manage on our own. We need other awesome individuals like *Gandhi, or a simple man in an orange vest,* to tame our egos and let our true lights shine.

TRANSITION – although she doesn't transition directly from the second to the third paragraph, she does transition quite well by referring to her thesis. *If trapped between the second and third paragraph, just transition with your thesis.*

DETAIL - appropriate level of detail.

THESIS CONNECTION – Love it! It's subtle, but clear.

Want to score a 6? Go that much deeper. She doesn't just stick to her thesis, but takes it to a new level here. Love that trick.

RELIST EXAMPLES – great!

RESTATEMENT of THESIS – great!

Introduction

This intro is short, sweet, to the point, and beautifully clear. I know exactly what her point of view is, and I know (as the reader) exactly where she is going to take me. She has a strong hook and flips direction with some elaboration that leads clearly to her thesis and subsequent list of examples. THIS is all you need to do!

Body Paragraph #1

She falters in this paragraph. She provides no transition, and I am not convinced she really knows all that much about Gandhi. The whole paragraph seems to be padded mainly with fluff. She does connect the example back to her thesis, which is key, so I am likely to forgive her if she can get back on track in body paragraph #2.

Body Paragraph #2

What is THIS, you ask: A clever way to make a personal example work. She falters with her historical example, but draws me right back in and hooks me with her personal one. I love the detailed description of the rain and the man. I love the dialogue. What a treat after reading 190 other essays about *The Great Gatsby!* At last! Something original! And the example PROVES her point. She connects it to her thesis (the man made her see that she has a good heart) and she takes her point of view a step further by acknowledging that we can't just depend on others to help us see ourselves, we also need to self-reflect. *Use your life, especially if you can't think of solid examples.* Did this really happen to my student? Hmm… I guess we'll never know, but I'm buying it.

Conclusion:

A two-sentence conclusion is just fine. (A one-sentence conclusion is also fine, if that is all you have time for.) She does everything she needs to do, except for add a concluding thought. She did have that extra thought at the end of the third paragraph, so I'm okay with the conclusion.

Where this essay is strong (the intro and body paragraph #2) it's strong, and when it's weak (body paragraph #1) it's weak, but overall it's going to get a score in the 10-12 range.

Don't let the essay discourage you. You are now a grammar whiz, so you know you've got that covered, and you now know the formula to follow to get a decent score on the essay. Prep those examples, practice on your own, and impress those readers with your solid skill!

Essay # 1 Practice

IMPORTANT: **USE A NO. 2 PENCIL. DO NOT WRITE OUTSIDE THE BORDER!**
Words written outside the essay box or written in ink **WILL NOT APPEAR**
in the copy sent to be scored, and your score will be affected.

Begin your essay on this page. If you need more space, continue on the next page.

Continue on the next page, if necessary.

Continuation of ESSAY Section 1 from previous page. Write below only if you need more space.
IMPORTANT: DO NOT START on this page - if you do, your essay may appear blank and your score may be affected.

Essay # 2 Practice

At the top of each practice page are instructions similar to what you'll see on the SAT.

IMPORTANT: **USE A NO. 2 PENCIL. DO NOT WRITE OUTSIDE THE BORDER!**
Words written outside the essay box or written in ink **WILL NOT APPEAR**
in the copy sent to be scored, and your score will be affected.

Begin your essay on this page. If you need more space, continue on the next page.

Continue on the next page, if necessary.

Chapter 8
Conclusion

Learning, digesting, and applying all 19-grammar rules can be overwhelming at first, but keep practicing and it should all start to gel together and click. Get a copy of the *College Board Official SAT Study Guide* and work through the practice tests. Remember, if you identify an error that doesn't fit within the parameters of one of the 19 grammar rules, then it probably isn't an error at all. You should always be able to state what is wrong, fix what is wrong, and justify with a grammar rule. Use the essay prompts in the College Board book to practice writing an essay in 25 minutes. Keep those pencils and that brain moving, follow the essay guidelines, and you are sure to score AT LEAST an 8 on the essay. Nothing to worry about!

Remember to take it easy the day before the test. Don't cram your brain full of new information. Do a light review, get a good night's sleep, and eat a power-packed breakfast.

Be confident and calm on test day so that your head remains clear. Take a couple of #2 pencils, and water and a snack to refuel during the break. If you find yourself confused and/or stressed, remember that you can always skip (and come back to) harder problems. In general, take a deep breath, believe in yourself, and remember the rules, definitions, and strategies I have taught you in this book. Good luck!